THE NAZI 'TT

HITLER'S 1939 PROPAGANDA
VICTORY ON THE ISLE OF MAN

ROGER WILLIS

*Dedicated to Leo Steinweg, a German motorcycle racer
who never made it to the TT*

ACKNOWLEDGEMENTS

EDITORIAL SOURCES

My greatest thanks go to Manx National Heritage's Manx Museum Library and its tremendously helpful staff, without whom the core research for this description of the events in 1939 – based on contemporary newspaper archives – would have been impossible. I have also relied extensively on marque histories and other historical volumes by Mick Walker, Ian Falloon, Raymond Ainscoe, Bob Holliday, Robert Cordon Champ, Roy Bacon, Roger Hicks, Eberhard Reuss, Richard Bassett, Martin Gilbert, Richard Gott, Dorothee Hochstetter and Mac McDiarmid, to whom I am indebted. On an individual level, I am grateful for the recollections, advice and help of Colin Appleyard, Walter Radcliffe, Heinz Herz, Dudley Robinson and Liz May. Last but not least, none of it would have happened without the untiring support of my in-house designer, production editrix and researcher Ruth Willis.

IMAGES

Undoubtedly the biggest contributions have come from Bill Snelling and his FoTTofinders archive, and Isle of Man Newspapers sports editor John Watterson, backed by Walter Radcliffe, Heinz Herz, Nick May, Mac McDiarmid, Das Bundesarchiv, US Federal Archives, Yad Vashem and Jeno Lempl. I thank them all.

ROGER WILLIS

Cover design by Ruth Willis. Cartography by Vic Bates.

CONTENTS

FOREWORD   5

I • WAR DRUMS ON THE GRID   7

II • THE EAGLE HAS LANDED   29

III • PHONEY WAR   53

IV • BLITZKRIEG   63

V • DON'T MENTION IT   81

VI • WE'LL MEET AGAIN   93

ISLE OF MAN TT COURSE MAP   103

THE 1989 BMW K.1.

50th ANNIVERSARY OF

SCHORSH MEIER'S

1939 T.T. WIN

◆ Back in days of yore, no function to which the dishevelled elite of British motorcycling journalism were invited was ever complete without bibulous excess and the grown-up equivalent of a goodie bag. In the case of BMW's gala dinner celebrating the 50th anniversary of the Nazi TT in 1989, the latter contained a collectable first-day cover (above) issued by the Isle of Man Post Office. And despite getting his nose in the gratis gargle trough, the author still managed to stagger around and collect autographs from the three surviving Senior TT leaderboard combatants. They're all history now, of course.

FOREWORD

It is now 70 years since Georg 'Schorsch' Meier won the Senior TT on a supercharged BMW – a double first of German rider and motorcycle. Understandably, BMW celebrated the 50th anniversary of this feat in 1989 by bringing Meier and his victorious machine back to the Isle of Man for a commemorative parade lap. There was also a gala dinner in his honour at what was then the Palace Hotel in Douglas, to which I was invited.

At that time I was a freelance journalist, having stepped down from my three-year reign as editor of *Bike* – then, as now, Britain's best-selling monthly motorcycle publication – in 1988. My professional excuse (if one was actually needed) for being at the 1989 TT was a short-term job as news presenter for the inaugural stand-alone Radio TT broadcasts on 1368AM by Manx Radio.

Those BMW festivities were the only interlude of light relief in what became a tragically fraught fortnight. I had to script and read on-air news reports of both the Chinese People's Liberation Army infamously massacring hundreds of civilians in Tiananmen Square and a grossly misconceived 1300cc Production race massacring some of the TT's finest exponents.

The deaths of Phil 'Mez' Mellor and Steve Henshaw in that race – plus Phil Hogg and sidecar passenger Marco Fattorelli in practice, and another sidecarist John Mulcahy in the races – dampened the spirits of everyone. But in the Palace's private dining room, media gloom was temporarily lifted by imbibing copiously at BMW's expense and reminiscing about the good old days. Schorsch Meier was joined at the top table by his 1939 team-mate and runner-up Jock West – in a wheelchair – and fourth place man Stanley Woods. Freddie Frith, who was third, had died a year earlier.

Meier was affable and relaxed, although somewhat uncommunicative because he couldn't speak much English. West was mostly unsmiling and taciturn, and it became evident as the evening wore on that he didn't cherish a very high opinion of Meier. Only Woods could be described as the life and soul of the party, still with an Irish twinkle in his eyes – even though his sight was almost gone by then.

Nevertheless, things progressed splendidly, and the only issue that intrigued me and one or two others was that there had been absolutely no mention of the war – until TT Riders Association supremo and journeyman race commentator Allan Robinson lurched to his feet as guest speaker. Robinson was a man who you either loved or hated – and I didn't love him. On this occasion my feelings were particularly justified because he tried to earn an Iron Cross to sit alongside his MBE, launching into a 'blood and glory' eulogy of heroic German efforts in 1939 which would have made the Führer proud.

I glanced across the room to see long-suffering BMW UK public relations manager Arthur Dalziel swivelling his gaze to the ceiling and shaking his head with incredulity as Robinson ranted on. I also noted with amusement that Mac McDiarmid, a TT racer and my successor as editor at *Bike* who shared a keen interest in thirst-quenching at such ligs, was outraged – and very close to heckling the speaker.

Afterwards, Dalziel poured PR oil on troubled waters and expressed BMW's corporate view, which went along the lines of 'they weren't really Nazis, it was just motorcycle sport'. So two decades later I set out to discover whether that was true. And it wasn't. Here is the real story, warts and all.

ROGER WILLIS,
PEEL, ISLE OF MAN • APRIL 2009

◆ NSKK-Korpsführer Adolf Hühnlein (right) presenting awards to SA paramilitary stormtroopers. A leading Nazi Party activist and close confidant of Hitler since the early 1920s, Hühnlein was instrumental in the politicisation and regimentation of German motorcycle sport through the creation of the Nationalsozialistische Kraftfahrkorps. NSKK insignia (above) subsequently appeared on the leathers of all German bike racers, apart from those who were already soldiers in the Reichswehr regular army. These Nazi paramilitary badges were conspicuous at the 1938 and 1939 Isle of Man TT races.

1 • WAR DRUMS ON THE GRID

To say that war drums had begun to beat during the Isle of Man TT in 1939 would be a gross understatement. Their sound had already been thunderous a year earlier when the 1938 event had taken place, and not-so-distant drumming had been audible for years. In fact, it is arguable that World War II was predictable and inevitable from the end of January 1933 when Adolf Hitler became Reichskanzler (Chancellor) of Germany and his Nationalsozialistische Deutsche Arbeiterpartei – the NSDAP or Nazi Party – was able to consolidate its power.

Just four days after being appointed Chancellor, Hitler is on record telling an introductory meeting of top German army and navy commanders that their country's key foreign policy objective would henceforth be the creation of Lebensraum – literally 'living space' – by any means necessary. From the very start, his plan was to remorselessly expand German borders by absorbing neighbouring countries.

And to imagine that the Nazis preferably intended to achieve this by peaceful diplomacy or democratic plebiscites would have been naive in the extreme. They already had a core modus operandi based on provoking anti-communist and anti-Jewish hysteria at home, backed up by consummate doses of well-organised ultraviolence thanks to the armed 'Brown Shirt' stormtroopers of their Sturmabteilung (SA) paramilitary wing to overwhelm democracy. That ethos, translated beyond Germany's borders – as history would prove – had to be military might was right in any sphere.

As 1933 progressed, Hitler pursued a ruthless campaign of suppression and downright murder against his political opponents until, on 14 July, the Nazi Party was declared the only legal political entity in Germany. His dictatorship was now almost absolute. And it became absolute the following year when the Weimar Republic's President Paul von Hindenburg died on 2 August 1934. Hitler promptly elevated himself from Führer of the Nazi Party to Führer of the Fatherland without recourse to electoral sanction, and so the Third Reich was born.

At the same time, the Nazis moved forward with an extraordinary transformation of German society into a totalitarian military-industrial complex dedicated to delivering Hitler's vision of a racially-pure Deutschland über alles. This extended to every aspect of life, including motorcycling and motorcycle sport, and the pivotal tool for this was the Nationalsozialistische Kraftfahrkorps (NSKK).

The NSKK grew out of the Nationalsozialistische Automobilkorps (NSAK) founded in 1930 by a veteran Nazi Party activist called Adolf Hühnlein, plus the SA-Kraftfahrwesens and SA-Motortrupps – both of which had been headed up by Hühnlein at various times. The primary task of these paramilitary subdivisions was to recruit drivers and their vehicles to transport detachments of SA stormtroopers to political rallies and frequent violent mass attacks on opponents. A former career officer in the German Imperial Army, Hühnlein's pedigree as a Nazi stalwart stretched right back to the beginning, basically commanding these SA thugs, defending Hitler and other Nazi Party bigwigs from hecklers at public meetings in the early 1920s. Along with the Führer, he was jailed for treasonable activities in the aftermath of the failed Munich 'beer hall putsch' in November 1923.

The NSAK became the NSKK in 1931 with a much broader remit that covered motorcycling as well and Hühnlein was appointed Korpsführer, still under the overall command of the SA. On the bike side, it initially used free

◆ Jewish-born DKW works rider Leo Steinweg (above) became the most high-profile victim of the NSKK paramilitary takeover of German motorcycle sport when he was refused a competition licence renewal at the end of 1933 because his ancestry was at odds with Nazi 'racial hygiene' regulations.

rider and motorcycle maintenance training as bait to attract recruits. After Hitler ordered the assassination of SA leader Ernst Röhm in 1934 and marginalised that organisation in favour of the SS, the NSKK absorbed the SA-Motortrupps and the Führer himself assumed supreme NSKK command. But really it became an adjunct of the Reichswehr regular army – generally known as the Wehrmacht – and the Waffen-SS, the full-on Nazi Party private army nurtured by Heinrich Himmler.

Before then, in September 1933, the NSKK's comparatively modest membership of around 10,000 received a huge boost when it took over all motoring and motorcycling clubs in Germany by government decree. It soon had half a million members. And that takeover also produced a consequence directly pertinent to subsequent appearances by German riders at the Isle of Man TT. At a stroke, the NSKK had seized control of German motor and motorcycle sport, including authorising the issue of national and international competition licences. The following year, NSKK-Korpsführer Hühnlein was thus elevated to the top job in the German motor and motorcycle sports authority too, variously described as Presidenten der Obersten Nationalen Sportbehörde für die Deutsche Kraftfahrt or Führer des Deutschen Kraftfahrsports.

So for the 1934 racing season onwards, all German motor and motorcycle sports competitors effectively had to be stormtroopers in the paramilitary NSKK – whether willing or otherwise – or regular military personnel to get a competition licence. And membership of either the NSKK or the armed forces was barred to 'non-Aryans' under Nazi racial hygiene regulations. For one German bike racing star, Leo Steinweg, this signalled the abrupt end of his career.

Leo Steinweg was a class act from Münster who was first contracted as a DKW factory rider in 1924 when he was only 18 years old. Such was his ongoing racing success in the 175cc and then 250cc classes that in 1929 he had invested the proceeds in a DKW motorcycle dealership specialising in race-tuned machines. But while his wife Emmy was an ethnic German, Steinweg – although a

Christian Catholic convert – had been born a Jew. Without a licence, he never raced again.

The bike shop survived until 1938, even though its customer base was progressively shrivelling because ever fewer Germans were prepared to patronise a concern which was obliged to identify itself as 'Jewish'. In the summer of that year, a former colleague who was by then a member of the SS tipped off Steinweg that his time was running out. So he managed to illegally dodge across the Dutch border at Gronau-Enschede on 1 September – just over two months before the SS-orchestrated Kristallnacht ('night of broken glass') pogrom was unleashed. In one appalling frenzy of brutality, 74 Jews were simply murdered in the streets. Large numbers of Jewish-owned businesses were also destroyed, nearly 200 synagogues burnt down and almost 30,000 Jews arrested for deportation to concentration camps.

Just as Steinweg was sacrificing his DKW works ride and racing career at the end of 1933 owing to his lack of racial hygiene, NSKK-Obertruppführer Ewald Kluge – who certainly knew of Steinweg and his predicament – was signed up by the DKW factory. A coincidence? Perhaps.

The NSKK-Motorsportschule, a dedicated training facility for car and bike racers established at Osterberg in 1936, became a major Nazi showcase often visited by big names in the Party and their guests. Off-road motorcycle racing in particular was seen as an excellent way to hone appropriate battlefield skills by the NSKK, as it developed into the principal feeder of already-trained despatch riders and bike mechanics to the Wehrmacht and Waffen-SS.

This emphasis on off-road capabilities meant many leading German motorcycle racers were multi-discipline performers. Most notably Georg 'Schorsch' Meier and Karl Gall – both members of the BMW team at the TT in 1938 and 1939 – had cut their racing teeth in arduous 1000-kilometre cross-country endurance trials (which we would now call enduros) that were popular in Germany during the late 1920s and early 1930s.

Meier was so successful in this type of event that he earned the nickname of Der Gusseiserne Schorsch – Cast

◆ Georg 'Schorsch' Meier during practice for the 1938 Isle of Man TT, complete with Eagle-and-Swastika Reichswehr army insignia on his leathers. Meier was the epitome of tough-guy modern German military motorcyclists with an impressive history of off-road competition success before he was persuaded to take up road racing. Legendarily dominant performances in gruelling 1000km enduros and the ISDT had already earned him the nickname of Der Guisseiserne Schorsch – Cast Iron Schorsch.

Iron Schorsch. Originally competing as part of the Bavarian State Police team, he attracted the attention of the Wehrmacht in 1934 after finishing a 1000km trial an hour ahead of his scheduled time on a complete nail of a bike. This was a BMW R4, a 400cc OHV single with a heavy pressed-steel riveted frame, rigid back end and deeply unfunctional pressed-steel trailing link front fork. Having transferred into the army as a military police motorcycle instructor, he went on to become Germany's star turn in its Trophy squad for the 1937 International Six Days Trial held in Wales that year, astride a rather more useful BMW 500cc boxer twin. Meier held the army rank of Feldwebel – a non-commissioned officer equivalent to the sergeant to sergeant major bracket in the British army.

The NSKK's mainstream motoring activities were predominantly geared towards assisting the mechanisation of the Wehrmacht by training truck drivers and mechanics. It's surprising to consider that the German army went to war with most of its supply-line logistics still dependent on horse-drawn wagons. In striking contrast to the technically-advanced armoured fighting vehicles up at the sharp end of Blitzkrieg action, their crews depended on a 19th-century mode of transport for supplies of fuel, ammunition and food until the NSKK got to work.

Returning to the Nazi Lebensraum recipe for global conflict, the timeline of key markers in the run-up to World War II was starting to get crowded. Hitler repudiated the Treaty of Versailles – with which Germany had been stitched up after losing the First World War – in 1935 and then comprehensively tore up any last vestige of it by marching the Wehrmacht in to reoccupy the demilitarised Rhineland buffer zone protecting the French border in March 1936. According to the Versailles and later 1925 Locarno treaties, the Rhineland was supposed to keep its demilitarised status permanently and any breach of this was to be regarded as 'a hostile act calculated to disturb the peace of the world'. But British and French occupation forces had actually withdrawn in 1930, so Hitler's audacious move met with no resistance apart from ineffectual bleating in Paris and London.

In Britain, the reaction to Hitler's rise to power and expansionist belligerence was characterised by essentially pacifist naivety, leading to rank appeasement from politicians like Stanley Baldwin and Neville Chamberlain, as well as varying degrees of sympathy and even outright admiration.

At the highest political level, memories of the slaughter of a generation of young men in the First World War trenches were fresh and few had the stomach for a replay. Prime Minister Baldwin reacted to the Rhineland reoccupation with tears in his eyes, claiming that the UK 'lacked the resources to enforce her treaty guarantees and that British public opinion would not stand for the use of military force anyway'. Lord Lothian dismissed it completely, famously remarking that 'it was no more than the Germans walking into their own backyard'. Only Winston Churchill rightly perceived the implicit menace. A lone voice relegated to the Conservative back benches in the House of Commons, he pointedly called for Anglo-French forces to spank the Germans back into obedience to their international treaty obligations. Nobody listened.

At the same time, fear of communism was a powerful and insidious influence. Both Hitler's Nazis in Germany and Benito Mussolini's similar National Fascist regime in Italy were avowedly anti-communist. While many people in Britain felt uncomfortable about aspects of these respective totalitarian states, they felt a lot more threatened by the prospect of Bolshevik rabble depriving them of their hard-earned property and privileges. They therefore tended towards the axiom that 'my enemy's enemy must be my friend'.

Anti-semitism was also regrettably still an acceptable sentiment in Britain in the 1930s. Hitler's attribution of blame on the Jews for every possible woe in German society had strong echoes picked up eagerly by many British ears as well. It's worth bearing in mind that such anti-Jewish prejudice wasn't finally illegalised in the UK until the Race Relations Act 1968 passed onto the statute books, 23 years after the nightmare of Hitler's 'Final Solution' to the Jewish problem was revealed. And similar legislation didn't come into effect on the Isle of Man until 2004!

Others took it much further – to covert or positively overt admiration of the Nazis. King Edward VIII, who was on the throne for most of 1936 before abdicating to avoid a constitutional crisis over his forthcoming marriage to American divorcee Wallis Simpson, was a secret pro-Nazi. As the Duke of Windsor after his abdication, he and his wife visited Germany as the personal guests of Hitler in 1937. And his later appointment to the British Military Mission in France was cut short because he was regarded as a security risk. He was ignominiously shuffled off to the Bahamas as Governor to keep him out of the way for the duration of the Second World War.

The unctuous American-born playboy Sir Henry 'Chips' Channon was another admirer, an appeaser widely suspected of deeper pro-Nazi sympathies. Channon married into the vastly wealthy Guinness brewing dynasty and became a naturalised British citizen, Conservative Member of Parliament for Southend and doyen of London high society in the 1930s. However, he spent more time batting for the other team than enjoying conjugal bliss with his wife, Lady Honor Guinness. Prince Paul of Yugoslavia – a Nazi stooge who banqueted with Hitler and was deposed by his ungrateful countrymen after signing the Tripartite Pact to join the Axis powers in 1941 – and the playwright Terence Rattigan numbered among his catamites. A close friend of Edward VIII, Channon was a supporter of Chamberlain's appeasement policies and thought the eventual declaration of war on Germany was a grievous error.

Most notoriously, Sir Oswald Mosley was so enamoured of the Nazis that he sought to emulate them. Mosley was a political gadfly who had been elected a Conservative MP in 1918 aged only 21 - the youngest member to take a seat in the House of Commons at that time. Within five years, he had crossed the floor of the house, first to sit as an independent and then join the Labour Party in 1924. He was appointed as a Minister without Portfolio responsible for tackling unemployment when Ramsay McDonald led Labour to its first-ever General Election victory in 1929. But he quickly became disenchanted and

◆ Karl Gall (facing page, left), seen here about to go out in practice week during the 1938 TT, was – like Meier – another veteran of the big off-road motorcycling marathons and mountain pass hill-climbs popular in Germany between the wars before taking up road racing. But Gall, who held the paramilitary rank of NSKK-Obertruppführer, was less successful on the Island and never actually started a race.

◆ The pro-Nazi Duke and Duchess of Windsor were feted as personal guests of Adolf Hitler in 1937 (above) after the Duke's abdication from the British throne. Treated as a major security risk just before and during the war, the former King Edward VIII was typical of many high-born closet Nazi sympathisers in Britain.

♦ Suitably uniformed and jackbooted home-grown 'führer' Sir Oswald Mosley (top) being hailed by his British Union of Fascists Blackshirt paramilitary stormtroopers at a rally in London. The BUF flag and insignia (above) sat comfortably alongside the Swastika and the organisation's battle hymn shared its tune with the Nazi Party Horst-Wessel-Lied anthem.

quit Labour to contest the 1931 General Election with his own New Party. This was an abject failure and so Mosley went to Italy to study the Mussolini phenomenon. He returned with the fiery zeal of a convert to the cause.

Mosley subsequently founded the British Union of Fascists in 1932 and attracted a disturbing level of support. With basically the same corporatist national socialism, anti-communism and anti-semitism agenda as the German Nazis and the Italian National Fascists, he soon had a claimed membership of more than 50,000 activists. And again emulating Hitler's Nazis, the BUF was quick to set up its own version of the SA stormtroopers, a paramilitary corps known colloquially as 'Blackshirts'. It also had a stirring official song to uplift the faithful, based closely on the Horst-Wessel-Lied Nazi Party anthem.

Apart from being an excuse for mincing around in Nazi-style uniforms and jackboots saluting each other, this organisation ostensibly provided security at BUF political rallies and meetings, which actually meant violently attacking and ejecting any hecklers. It also fought regular blood-spattered skirmishes with communist, anarchist and Jewish groups on the streets. The most famous of these occurred in October 1936 when the Blackshirts tried to march through the then predominantly Jewish East London borough of Stepney. Despite considerable help from the police, they were bludgeoned to a halt in what came to be known as the Battle of Cable Street.

As well as sympathisers in high places – Mosley was yet another chum of King Edward VIII – he also had powerful press connections. *Daily Mail* proprietor Lord Rothermere, a fairly blatant pro-Nazi, was a major backer. Rothermere both provided initial funding for the BUF and ensured supportive propaganda in his newspaper. One memorable *Daily Mail* front-page banner headline trumpeted 'Hurrah for the Blackshirts'. The *Daily Mirror* was also an early supporter. However, as the war approached and BUF activities became steadily more disreputable in the public eye, this popular press backing withered away.

The BUF and its leader enjoyed a decidedly cosy

relationship with the Nazi hierarchy in Germany, though – which may have extended to financial help. Sir Oswald Mosley married his second wife, Diana Mitford, at a secret wedding in the Berlin home of Nazi Party propaganda supremo Joseph Goebbels on 6 October 1936. Apart from Goebbels and his wife Magda, the only other guest at these nuptials was Adolf Hitler – who modestly presented the happy couple with a silver-framed photograph of himself.

Diana Mitford and her sister Unity, two of the daughters of Lord Redesdale, were deeply-smitten Nazi groupies who first went to Germany in 1933 to attend the Nuremberg Rally of Victory celebrating Hitler's seizure of power. This lavish martial event was made into a movie, Der Sieg des Glaubens (The Victory of the Faith) by noted German film director Leni Riefenstahl. Unity, who was only 19 years old, promptly struck up a warm friendship with Hitler - the intimacy of which is a matter for conjecture. The Mitford sisters returned to Nuremberg for the next four years' worth of such goose-stepping jamborees. The Führer also laid on a chauffeur-driven Merc limo for Diana's personal convenience at the Berlin Olympic Games in 1936.

Anyway, the sorry collection of cowards and collaborators who comprised much of Britain's political establishment during the 1930s continued to turn a blind eye to what Winston Churchill would later describe as the risk of 'sinking into the abyss of a new Dark Age'. And then the next portion of Lebensraum application arrived – less than three months before the 1938 TT.

The 'Anschluss' annexation of Austria into a Greater Germany on 12 March of that year was another simple, smooth and almost effortless operation. Following a spate of destabilising threats to Austrian Chancellor Kurt Schuschnigg in February, Hitler manoeuvred Schuschnigg into resigning on 11 March – thus allowing the Austrian Nazi Party to carry out a coup d'état to maintain order and 'avoid bloodshed'. The Wehrmacht's 8th Army marched in the next morning at their invitation, without any resistance. They were in fact greeted by cheering Austrians giving 'Heil Hitler' salutes. The Führer himself drove by car across the

◆ The Nazi Party's huge, choreographed Rally of Victory at Nuremberg in 1933 (above) was attended by upper-class Hitler groupie Diana Mitford – who later married British Union of Fascists leader Sir Oswald Mosley – and her younger sister Unity. This stirring occasion and the company they were keeping there made them so moist that they returned for repeated doses.

◆ After invading Austria in March 1938, Germans invaded the Isle of Man too at the end of May in their first major coordinated assault on the TT. At least the Manx public knew this wasn't a purely sporting enterprise and quickly labelled them 'the Nazis'. They were led by a trio of riders mounted on BMW 255 Kompressor supercharged boxer twins – the fastest racing motorcycles ever seen on the Island at that time. Jock West, a token British rider in the German Senior TT squad, is seen here howling through Union Mills on one of them.

border that afternoon and began a grand tour of the country culminating in a triumphant welcome from more than 200,000 newly-recruited German citizens upon his arrival in Vienna on 2 April. Austria had already been declared the German province of Ostmark on 13 March.

The treaties of Versailles and St Germain specifically prohibited the union of Austria and Germany, but that didn't make the slightest difference. The UK and French governments sat on their hands, probably to stop them from shaking. Although arch-appeaser Neville Chamberlain, who had taken over from Baldwin as British Prime Minister, issued 'grave warnings' to Germany via his Foreign Secretary and subsequently through the British Ambassador in Berlin, he didn't do anything more concrete. 'The hard fact is that nothing could have arrested what has actually happened unless this country and other countries had been prepared to use force,' Chamberlain plaintively told the House of Commons. And at that point Britain most certainly wasn't prepared. At least he did order a defence review that sowed the seeds of urgent rearmament and mobilisation the following year.

But attitudes were changing. While the British government dithered, British public opinion was waking up to the threat from Germany. This was self-evident on the Isle of Man at the 1938 TT in June. Both the Manx local newspapers and the UK motorcycling press had begun to describe German competitors as 'the Nazis'. They had also noticed that there were more of them, and they were both better-organised and better-equipped.

This invasion of a pair of three-man squads, one mounted on awesome BMW 255 Kompressor supercharged twins for the blue-riband Senior and the other on howling works DKW supercharged two-strokes – possibly the noisiest motorcycles ever to assault the Island – in the Lightweight, was the talk of the town in practice week. Of the four German riders, one was a regular soldier and the other three were NSKK paramilitary troopers – two of which held the superior ranks of NSKK-Obertruppführer and NSKK-Sturmführer.

◆ British Prime Minister Neville Chamberlain (above, left), as chief architect of Britain's abject appeasement policy, somehow believed that Hitler could be persuaded to compromise for the sake of peace – despite repeated evidence to the contrary. If he had stood up to the Third Reich and opted for rearmament much earlier, the Führer's domestic political hegemony would have been fatally weakened and history might have followed a very different course.

The Senior challenge was the most feared. British rider Jock West had finished sixth as a lone factory BMW-mounted entry in the previous year's race, only robbed of a better placing by his leaking fuel tank in the closing stages. And for 1938 he was joined by the German star pairing of Georg Meier and Karl Gall.

The BMW 255 Kompressor was highly advanced for the era, a DOHC supercharged 'boxer' flat-twin, a pure racing motorcycle that had virtually nothing in common with the manufacturer's production machines. By 1938, the Kompressor was producing almost 60bhp. Full works Manx Nortons of the period struggled to reach 50bhp. It also featured another novelty – hydraulically-damped front telescopic forks. The factory Nortons had teleforks too for the first time in 1938 but they were undamped pogo sticks.

As a result of all this technology, speed-trap times during practice on the Sulby Straight – clocked between Cooil Deane and Cushag Cottage – were pretty astonishing. West registered a stupendous 130.4mph with Meier second at 121.6mph. Gall was down in sixth spot on 118.4mph behind the three factory Norton singles of John 'Crasher' White, Harold Daniell and Freddie Frith respectively running at 121.4mph, 120.8mph and 119.2mph.

◆ A determined Jock West (above) in the 1938 TT paddock. West, who worked for the British BMW importer, already had one top-ten TT finish on the Kompressor in 1937 and was faster than his two German team-mates in 1938 practice. However, imparting his experience to TT rookies Meier and Gall was deemed more important to the factory than the potential embarrassment of facilitating Senior TT victory for a British rider over true sons of the Fatherland. As it turned out, none of them won that year.

The 1938 250cc two-stroke DKW was also a very clever purpose-built racing tool, a rotary-valve supercharged 'split single' with a 30bhp power output. Again this gave it a considerable advantage over the opposition, which basically consisted of modified four-stroke road bikes. So the Lightweight speed-trap leaderboard was equally breathtaking with Ewald Kluge's DKW screaming through Sulby at 107.8mph and his team-mate Siegfried 'Sissi' Wünsche following at 104mph. Kluge was a full 13mph faster than third-placed Harold Hartley riding a 250cc Rudge single.

Moving into race week, Wednesday's Lightweight TT had been postponed for two hours due to fog on the Mountain and then eventually ran in very windy conditions. The DKWs were odds-on favourites, especially given that Italian 1937 winner Omobono Tenni and the works

Moto Guzzi team hadn't entered. But not everything went according to plan.

Wünsche, on the second-fastest DKW in practice, seized and stopped at Ginger Hall on his first lap, and was later reported to be touring into Ramsey. Kluge, however, was riding like a man possessed. From a standing start, he broke Tenni's 1937 lap record by 29 seconds at 79.04mph. His English DKW team-mate Ernie Thomas was behind him, 54 seconds in arrears.

◆ NSKK-Sturmführer Ewald Kluge (above), who'd had his application for coveted full Nazi Party membership accepted a year earlier, screams through Quarterbridge during a memorable charge in the 1938 Lightweight TT. He broke Omobono Tenni's Lightweight record on his first circuit from a standing start and then did it again second time around, putting in the first 80mph-plus lap ever achieved by a 250cc machine on the TT Mountain Course.

◆ Siegfried 'Sissi' Wünsche (above) had claimed an impressive fifth place in the previous year's Lightweight TT for DKW during his first visit to the Island, with his more-experienced British team-mate Ernie Thomas on the podium in third. But although he had been second-fastest behind Kluge in 1938 practice, he never completed a single lap in the race. His bike seized at Ginger Hall.

20

On the next lap, Kluge did it again, beating Tenni's record by 58 seconds at 80.35mph – the first 80mph-plus lap on a 250cc bike. Thomas hung on to the runner-up spot to make it a DKW one-two but, on his third circuit, ran out of petrol at Brandish, free-wheeled to Hillberry and then pushed in – effectively out of contention. Kluge just kept on charging, now five and a half minutes ahead of Excelsior-mounted Ginger Wood.

By the time he came in for fuel for the second time at the end of his fifth lap, he had nine minutes in hand, and then maintained a blistering pace to pull out an advantage of more than 11 minutes after his final two laps. Kluge's average lap time over the entire seven laps was actually 18 seconds quicker than Tenni's lap record of the previous year. Not surprisingly, the German contingent at the Grandstand went wild with joy, celebrating their first-ever TT victory.

In the Senior stakes on Friday, the weather was fine and warm, and an additional 12,000 day excursionists had stepped off steamers in Douglas harbour that morning to join the vast crowds already lining the Mountain Course. But the Nazi threat had already began to retreat before the race.

Kurt Gall was a non-starter, having been found badly injured in a ditch above the 26th Milestone on the Tuesday morning of race week as a result of crashing during an unofficial open-roads practice session – apparently riding the wrong way round the course when he binned it. And then as riders roared off from the Grandstand, Meier's luck also ran out. His mechanic had replaced soft warm-up spark plugs in the starting queue and stripped the thread on one cylinder. Cast Iron Schorsch found himself riding a suddenly single-pot bike down Bray Hill and pulled off at the bottom. Only Jock West was still in the running, and finally finished a creditable fifth.

Instead of another victory for the Third Reich, the Nazis then had to witness an epic battle between Britain's finest, billed by the press as 'History's most dramatic Senior TT' in which 'Daniell shuts the lions' mouths'.

◆ The banshee wail of Ewald Kluge's supercharged two-stroke split-single probably frightened a lot of sheep as he exited Windy Corner up on the Mountain (above). His extraordinary performance continued unabated throughout the 1938 Lightweight, extending his lead over runner-up Ginger Wood to more than 11 minutes at the chequered flag. Grabbing Germany's first-ever TT victory for both man and machine in such emphatic Aryan-superhero style made him into a very popular Nazi back home.

◆ As sole BMW factory rider left in contention in the 1938 Senior after Gall was sidelined by a practice crash and Meier broke down yards from the start, Jock West delivered a fine mercenary performance for his Nazi sponsors to take fifth spot. And it has to be said his result would have been considerably better if the speed of his pit stops had matched British rivals – and German mechanics were to blame for that. But it's doubtful if anybody could have taken Norton-mounted Harold Daniell's glory away from him – bearing in mind that the outright 90.99mph record he set was unbeaten in 1939 and stood for 12 years.

In a race first led by Freddie Frith and then Velocette-mounted Stanley Woods, Harold Daniell gradually worked his way up from a distant fourth spot to run neck-to-neck with Frith at the end of lap five, only three seconds behind Woods. And at that point in the closing stages, Daniell must have experienced some kind of epiphany, because he managed to wind his Norton up to deliver the first-ever TT lap of under 25 minutes – 90.75mph – on his sixth circuit and take the lead by five seconds.

Then just to make sure he was home and dry, his seventh and final lap was even faster – a sensational 24 minutes and 52.6 seconds, an average of 90.99mph that was to stand as the outright TT record for 12 years. Having broken the race and outright lap records twice, Daniell won by 15.2 seconds with an average race speed of 89.11mph. So it was most definitely Union Jacks rather than Swastikas waving at the end, as Britannia ruled the roads.

NSKK-Obertruppführer Karl Gall spent four months recovering from his injuries – a badly broken arm and severe concussion – in Ramsey Cottage Hospital on the Isle of Man that year and was finally repatriated to Germany in October 1938. By then, Hitler had upped his Lebensraum game considerably and the unfortunate Gall went home to a bigger country – that now included a substantial chunk of what had been Czechoslovak territory.

The Nazis had set about their plan to suck Czechoslovakia into the Reich much earlier that year. Hitler's ploy was based on 'protecting' the rights of the ethnically German majority population in an area known as Sudetenland. This was the border region of the old kingdom of Bohemia, part of the Hapsburg Austro-Hungarian empire until its collapse at the end of the First World War. Some 23.4 per cent of the total Czech population were ethnically German, according to a census carried out in 1921 after the country was created, and were mainly concentrated in Sudetenland. Political activists among them, latterly led by the proto-Nazi Sudetendeutsche Partei (SDP), had been campaigning for unification with Germany ever since the early 1920s and the SDP's increasingly shrill calls for

'justice' provided the Nazis with a very convenient excuse for the involvement they desired.

The British government had already been wringing its hands in ineffectual despair in May 1938, before the TT. While warning the sabre-rattling Germans against military intervention in public, Prime Minister Chamberlain had also been obsequiously leaning on the Czech government in Prague to make concessions. Although Britain had no treaty obligations to the Czechs, the Franco-Czechoslovak Alliance signed in 1924 nevertheless dragged it into the loop. Because Britain was formally allied to France, if the French mobilised forces to support the Czechs, the British would be duty-bound to get involved too – and that is exactly what Chamberlain was most worried about.

◆ While the bikes Kluge and Wünsche rode in 1938 received careful scrutineering from TT authorities (top), with the DKW factory mechanics looking rather stressed, less attention was paid to their underlying political propaganda role that year – which would become more blatant in 1939.

◆ In the 1938 Lightweight TT winner's enclosure, NSKK paramilitary insignia on Ewald Kluge's leathers clearly stands out. The corpulent gentleman on the left with an avuncular hand on his shoulder is Adolf Meurer, race director of DKW parent Auto Union – a fellow enthusiastic Nazi Party member.

In August 1938 intelligence information reached the British that Germany was mobilising Wehrmacht reservists and intended to invade Czechoslovakia in September. When this news was passed on to Czech President Edvard Benes, he caved in and conceded most of the SDP's autonomy demands, potentially undermining Hitler's excuse for aggressive action. But extremists in Sudetenland scuppered any deal by provoking violence against the Czech police, which led to an imposition of martial law.

Chamberlain then flew to Germany on 15 September for a meeting with Hitler at Berchtesgaden. There, he offered to push the Czechs into agreeing to Nazi demands for the annexation of any areas where more than half of the population was ethnic German. Hitler apparently went along with this simply because he didn't believe the Czech government would play ball. However, under intense pressure from the British and French, Benes finally agreed.

But when Chamberlain returned to Germany seven days later for a summit at Bad Godesberg to sort out the details of a peaceful transfer of disputed Sudetenland territory, he discovered that Hitler had moved the goalposts and now required its surrender with no further interference by 28 September. However, the Führer then changed his mind about unilateral Nazi military intervention, having realised he could bluff his way through more cheaply. So he agreed to a further summit, notionally suggested by Italian Fascist dictator Benito Mussolini.

This duly took place in Munich on 30 September and was attended by Hitler, Mussolini, Chamberlain and French prime minister Edouard Daladier. Czech government representatives were not invited. The four of them were presented with a face-saving document supposedly drafted by Mussolini but in fact drawn up by veteran Nazi potentate Hermann Göring. This was the 'Munich Agreement', the piece of paper farcically waved by Chamberlain to an adulatory crowd as he descended the steps of his aircraft at Heston aerodrome back in England. He promised the assembled throng that it guaranteed 'peace for our time'. Actually, it conceded all of Hitler's demands with immediate effect. Vociferous British parliamentary opponents of this shabby deal, led by Winston Churchill and Anthony Eden, were cynically labelled 'warmongers' in the Nazi press. The Wehrmacht rolled across the Czech border to occupy Sudetenland the next day – and would subsequently invade the rest of Czechoslovakia six months later in March 1939.

This may have been Britain's feeblest hour of appeasement but the writing was inescapably on the wall and even idiots could hear the war drums now. Reluctant as he had been to countenance large-scale British rearmament for most of his early tenure of 10 Downing Street, Chamberlain had finally admitted that it was imperative late in 1938.

To be fair, as Chancellor of the Exchequer in 1936 and later Prime Minister, Chamberlain had pushed through some defence expenditure increases. But these were based on a non-offensive strategy that paralleled appeasement, and were also hamstrung by the parlous state of the British economy and its industrial capabilities after the Great Depression. Their nature was expressed through a 'Limited-Liability' doctrine in 1937, that assumed commitment of land forces in continental Europe could be avoided. So the Army budget was slashed further and savings redirected towards the Royal Navy and – to the greatest extent – the Royal Air Force.

Chamberlain still wasn't convinced though. 'How horrible, how fantastic that we should be digging trenches and trying on gas masks here because of a quarrel in a faraway country between people of whom we know nothing,' he said in a BBC radio broadcast on 27 September 1938. 'I am myself a man of peace from the depths of my soul.'

But history was rapidly overtaking Chamberlain's high-minded pacifism. Reliable intelligence reported that Hitler was comprehensively gearing up for war. The RAF had already begun to draw up lists of potential bomber targets in Germany earlier in 1938 and by the end of the year plans were afoot to move a couple of token British Army divisions to France.

And then, in January 1939, the British government received a report that an imminent German invasion of the Netherlands was about to take place, so that the Luftwaffe

could use Dutch airfields to launch a knock-out strategic bombing offensive against British cities. This completely false story had been planted by the German Abwehr military intelligence head Admiral Wilhelm Canaris, a man who will reappear further into this book with a surprising connection to the Isle of Man TT. The enigmatic Canaris had – quite deliberately it later transpired – done Hitler no favours. What he actually achieved was a complete volte-face in British defence policy.

However, real moves by the Nazis were under way. Military planning for a German invasion of Poland began on 3 April on Hitler's orders. And then later that month he cleared the diplomatic decks for action by renouncing both the Anglo-German Naval Agreement and the German-Polish Non-Aggression Pact.

The race was now on to get tooled up as fast as possible. Chamberlain committed to sending a large expeditionary force to France and guaranteed French territorial integrity against German aggression, along with that of Switzerland, Belgium and the Netherlands. To this end, he ordered an immediate and enormous military expansion. The Territorial Army reservist force promptly began recruitment to take its strength from 13 to 26 divisions. And in April – only two months in advance of the TT – legislation was passed to introduce military conscription to massively bolster the regular army too – something that had never happened before in what was still theoretically 'peacetime' – with conscripts due to be called up that summer. Many TT visitors and some riders would be wearing khaki uniforms and carrying rifles barely a month after the event.

British industry was also put on a war footing to equip this huge increase in the armed forces, with factories turning over their production to military contracts. One of these was Norton, which concentrated all of its capabilities on churning out decidedly slow 16H side-valve singles for the army rather than sporting motorcycles. As a result, it announced there would be no Norton works entry at the forthcoming 1939 Isle of Man TT races.

◆ Axis leaders Benito Mussolini and Adolf Hitler (top) ran diplomatic rings around the British and French in the run-up to World War II. The most notorious example of this took place at the Munich Conference, where Neville Chamberlain and French premier Edouard Daladier (above left and second left) ignominiously surrendered Czechoslovakia to the Germans without a shot fired in pursuit of 'peace for our time'. While all this was going on, dedicated Nazis like Ewald Kluge (facing page, left) just carried on racing for the Reich.

2 • THE EAGLE HAS LANDED

It is now hard to comprehend what atmosphere of foreboding must have weighed down the 1939 Isle of Man TT races. Fear and loathing was in the air with Churchill's blood, toil, tears and sweat just around the corner. And then a disciplined phalanx of German competitors – representing the nation with which Britain was about to go to war three months later – disembarked onto the quayside in Douglas.

They were the crème de la crème of Third Reich motorcycling talent with two reigning European champions – Georg Meier and Ewald Kluge, respectively in the 500 and 250 classes – among them, split into three squads under BMW, DKW and NSU battle standards. As for weaponry, they were equipped with thoroughbred full-works racing machines featuring the very latest technology. No expense had been spared in the pursuit of victory.

Although it wasn't immediately apparent then, they undoubtedly constituted a highly-political propaganda exercise, conceived and sponsored by the Nazi state and run on a paramilitary basis. If a global conflict of unimaginable savagery was about to ensue, this was more than just a rehearsal for combat. It was an early skirmish.

The titular head of this daunting force was Baron Fritz von Faulkenhayn. And he was certainly hailed as such by the Manx who – then as now – sadly love to tug their collective forelock to nobility. A Fokker fighter pilot during the First World War and personal friend and comrade in arms of 'Red Baron' Manfred von Richtofen – the most successful air ace in that war – Falkenhayn was a fully-paid-up Prussian aristocrat with interesting antecedents.

His father, Generaloberst Baron Erich von Falkenhayn, was already an infamous memory throughout Europe. Falkenhayn Senior, who died in 1922, had been Chief of Staff of the German Imperial Army for most of the First World War and Minister of War in Kaiser Wilhelm II's Prussian government for part of it.

He was best-known for two things. As the 'Blood Miller' of Verdun, he had presided over the single most murderous episode of the First World War, which was conceived by him as a 'self-sustaining killing ground' to annihilate the French army rather than a means towards the taking of any geographical military objective. Considerably more than a million French and German soldiers died fighting over the Verdun salient during the 11 months of this action (which ultimately failed). And then, of course, Erich von Falkenhayn will be credited for all eternity as the man who introduced chlorine gas in particular, and poison gas warfare in general, as the first true weapon of mass destruction. Eat your heart out, Saddam Hussein.

The Falkenhayn family also had a decidedly seamy side. Fritz's cousin Richard was a member of the Nazi Gestapo secret police who implicated his own ex-wife Benita in a spy scandal during 1934. Swiss-born Benita von Falkenhayn was a blonde Berlin party animal who, along with her friend Renate von Natzmer, had been involved in a troilist love affair with a former officer in the Polish Legion of the Austro-Hungarian army called Jerzy Sosnowski. In reality, Sosnowski still covertly held the rank of major, because he was a military intelligence agent for Poland. The two women were arrested following a Gestapo raid on an orgiastic soirée in Sosnowski's apartment at which Richard von Falkenhayn had also been present.

◆ Reichswehr Feldwebel Georg 'Schorsch' Meier (facing page, left) returned to the Isle of Man for the 1939 Senior TT as reigning European 500cc champion.

◆ The Nazi Party's most-feted motorcycling member and reigning 250cc
European champion NSKK-Stürmführer Ewald Kluge (above) also returned to
the Island in 1939 to defend his Lightweight TT title from the previous year.
In addition, he was due to contest the Junior TT for the first time on a 350cc
supercharged split-twin version of the howling DKW two-stroke.

30

Whether or not they were both actually involved in anything more than three-in-a-bed romps with the dodgy Pole spook remains a mystery, because their trial for espionage and treason was held in secret – although Natzmer did work in the Reichswehr military headquarters and had access to classified information. But the verdict of the court and the sentence it decreed became public knowledge – guilty as charged and death.

On 18 February 1935 Benita von Falkenhayn and Renate von Natzmer were executed in Berlin's Plotzensee prison, taking their places in history as the last subjects of judicially-sanctioned beheading by axe in Europe. The executioner, Karl Gröpler, wore the traditional tailcoat, top hat and white gloves while carrying out his duties. Hitler subsequently abolished this method in favour of guillotine and gallows. However, Himmler's SS prison warders sometimes employed cheese wire in hangings, rather than rope, to add an amusing retro decapitation twist.

Despite being sentenced to incarceration for the rest of his life, Jerzy Sosnowski was repatriated to Poland after only 14 months in a prisoner exchange. Such untypical mercy was soon put in context. The Polish authorities arrested, tried and eventually convicted him as a double-agent – coincidentally at the end of TT race week in 1939. The Gestapo had successfully turned Sosnowski around. This time he didn't get out and is believed to have died in a Soviet jail about ten years later.

Getting back to Baron Fritz on the Isle of Man, his official status there was as managing director of the NSU motorcycle factory at Neckarsulm near Stuttgart in southern Germany. Falkenhayn had joined the struggling NSU concern as sales director in 1930 and got the top job two years later when the company was relaunched from bankruptcy and refinanced through the sale of its automotive manufacturing operations to Fiat.

He soon became a keen exponent of the Nazi corporatist political strategy of making cheap motorised transport accessible to the broad mass of the German public, to nurture popular support. On two wheels, the biggest

◆ Baron Erich von Falkenhayn (above), father of NSU managing director Baron Fritz von Falkenhayn, had been Chief of Staff of the German Imperial Army for most of the First World War and is still notorious both as the man behind that conflict's bloodiest battle at Verdun and his introduction of poison gas as a weapon of mass destruction. The medal at his throat is the 'Blue Max', the highest military award in the Reich until the Nazis introduced their Iron Cross.

contributions towards this aim from NSU came with the budget-priced NSU-D Quick, a 98cc two-stroke motorcycle-styled moped capable of about 35mph, and similarly inexpensive NSU-D Pony two-stroke motorcycle models in 98cc, 175cc and 201cc configurations. The Quick was Germany's best-selling bike from its launch in 1936 until the war, and more than 230,000 were made during its production life – which resumed after the war.

Falkenhayn also worked with Ferdinand Porsche at the personal behest of the Führer to originate the Type 32 prototype of Hitler's vision of a Volkswagen (people's car) in 1934. However, after Fiat pointed out that NSU had made legally-binding undertakings to refrain from car production after selling that side of its interests, development was moved on from Neckarsulm.

Ironically, British motorcycle designer Walter William Moore played a crucial role in NSU's recovery under Baron von Falkenhayn. Moore had been recruited in 1929 from Norton – where he had been most notably responsible for the bevel-driven overhead-camshaft CS1 racing forerunner of the all-conquering Manx Norton.

Moore's first project for his new German masters was an OHC four-stroke racing single, the NSU 'Bullus' 500 SS unveiled in 1930. This was so reminiscent of the Norton CS1 that British commentators sourly joked that NSU stood for 'Norton Spares Used'. However, in the hands of English

expatriate Tom Bullus – whose name became inextricably linked to the bike – it made an immediate impression in German national and European racing.

Bullus, a big Yorkshire lad from Bradford, already had some good TT results under his belt – fourth on a Panther in the 1925 Senior and fifth on a factory Sunbeam in the 1930 Senior – when he moved to Germany with fresh ink on a NSU works contract. He went on to take fourth spot in the 1930 German Grand Prix at the Nürburgring for NSU, and beat all-comers in the high-profile Alpine mountain events that year. Bullus set a new outright record for the daunting 21.5km charge over the Klausen Pass and also won the similar Gaisburg event near Salzburg in Austria, besides victories at Monza and the Schottenring back in Germany.

◆ NSU's pedigree on the Isle of Man was established in the mid-1930s when Oskar Steinbach (facing page, left) campaigned the factory's 'Bullus' OHC four-stroke singles in the 1935 and 1936 TT races. Steinbach is portrayed here on the Island in 1936. This bike was designed by former Norton engineer Walter Moore and widely mocked by the British for its similarity to the CS1 Manx Norton forerunner. The standard joke was that NSU stood for 'Norton Spares Used'. Moore also designed more mundane – and profitable – two-stroke motorcycles for NSU that had no Norton associations. These included the 98cc NSU-D Quick (above left), which became Germany's best-selling bike, and the NSU-D Pony (above right) in a range of capacity configurations.

◆ NSKK-Korpsführer Adolf Hühnlein, Reichsführer Adolf Hitler and NSKK-Obergruppenführer Erwin Kraus (above, left to right) meeting in Germany during the late 1930s. Paramilitary uniforms were always worn on home soil but never abroad. When Kraus was sent on his command mission to the Isle of Man TT in 1939, he was masquerading as a senior civilian representative of the German equivalent of Britain's Auto-Cycle Union racing authority.

The following year he won again at Gaisberg and at the Hungarian Grand Prix, and came second at Monza. And in 1932 he won the first bike race held at the new Hockenheim circuit. There is still a street in Hockenheim called Tom-Bullus-Strasse.

Tom Bullus married Hilde Gehr, the daughter of a NSU director, and retired from racing at the end of 1932 – at the behest of his new father-in-law. He continued to work for NSU for a while until, as the war approached, he moved back to Bradford to set up a motorcycle dealership with his brother. In the 1950s and 1960s, he was well-known around the Yorkshire motorcycle trade as manager of Union Transport Finance, a hire-purchase company based in Pudsey. He later moved to head up another finance business in Bradford before finally retiring to Harrogate, where he died in the 1990s.

In 1935, Oskar Steinbach used 350 and 500 versions of Moore's SS to take both classes in the German national championship. Steinbach (who is mistakenly described as 'Otto' in Manx competitor records) also did well at the TT for NSU, coming fifth in the 1935 Senior on a 500 and sixth in the 1936 Junior on a 350.

But nobody could claim that the hugely successful utilitarian two-stroke Quick and Pony machines – also designed by Walter Moore – were Norton knock-offs. And then in 1938 he and his assistant Albert Röder, who became NSU's chief designer after the war, also created the advanced NSU DOHC supercharged twins that debuted on the Island at the 1939 TT.

By 1938, NSU had overtaken DKW as the largest motorcycle manufacturer in Germany and was one of the biggest in the world, producing more than 60,000 bikes annually. That made Fritz von Falkenhayn into a leading Nazi industrialist. And, if nothing else, his presence on the Island in 1939 signified how important the TT was to Third Reich propaganda. But for all his professional prominence Falkenhayn was just the front man, because NSKK-Obergruppenführer Erwin Kraus was really in charge of the stormtroops – even if he wasn't actually in uniform.

He was described by the Manx press as Herr E Kraus, representative of the German equivalent of the Auto-Cycle Union - the Obersten Nationalen Sportbehörde für die Deutsche Kraftfahrt (ONS). But this, of course, was now effectively just an administrative satellite of the paramilitary Nationalsozialistische Kraftfahrkorps, with NSKK-Korpsführer Adolf Hühnlein at the helm. Kraus was his second-in-command at both the NSKK and ONS. And, like Hühnlein, he was among the top elite of the Nazi Party. The pair of them often made public appearances together with Hitler at motorsport presentations and events.

Of the eight German factory riders on the Island, six were NSKK stormtroopers and therefore under the direct command of Kraus. The other two, Siegfried Wünsche and Georg Meier, were both regular soldiers in the Wehrmacht but would have readily deferred to him – although Meier's leathers carried the simple Reichswehr Eagle-and-Swastika insignia rather than the fancier NSKK version.

The DKW team had three German riders – Ewald Kluge, Siegfried 'Sissi' Wünsche and Heinrich 'Heiner' Fleischmann. Kluge, apart from being the 'officer-class' NSKK-Stürmführer among them, had plenty of Isle of Man experience given this was his third TT visit. He had made his debut in the 1937 Lightweight on the older reed-valve version of the DKW supercharged split-single and diced for the lead in the early stages with Stanley Woods before breaking down. More famously, he had then absolutely cleared off in the 1938 Lightweight on the more reliable and powerful rotary-valve bike.

Born in Lausa – between Leipzig and Dresden – in 1909, Ewald Kluge was the product of a difficult and deprived childhood. His mother died when he was only 12 years old and he had to leave school and take a succession of menial jobs to help his father make ends meet. He was made redundant from the most promising of these, as a trainee motor mechanic, as Germany plunged into economic crisis in 1928 but then found work as a taxi driver in Dresden.

Kluge's motorcycle racing career began in 1929 after he bought a British-made Dunelt and entered a road race at

◆ DKW had been contesting the Lightweight TT with various versions of its supercharged two-stroke single since 1935, when Oskar Steinbach, Arthur Geiss – that year's German 250 champion - and Walfried Winkler came to the Island. Steinbach returned the following year (above) with Geiss as his teammate. They were replaced by Ewald Kluge, Siegfried Wünsche and Britain's Ernie Thomas in the DKW TT squad for 1937.

◆ Siegfried Wünsche was on his third visit to the Isle of Man in 1939.
During his Lightweight debut in 1937 (above) it is worth noting that NSKK
paramilitary insignia had yet to appear on riders' leathers, even though they
were all members. But if the Nazi propaganda element wasn't then thrust to
the fore, DKW certainly took its TT effort seriously – signalled by the presence
of Auto Union race director Adolf Meurer (above, second from right)

nearby Freiberg, finishing an impressive third behind a pair of factory DKWs. He then competed as a privateer using DKW machinery, until DKW signed him up in 1933 as a reserve rider for the 1934 season. He got a full works contract in 1935 and became German national 250cc road-racing champion for the next three years from 1936 to 1938 and European champion too in 1938.

Like many NSKK motorcycle stormtroopers, Kluge was also an extremely competent off-road rider – a gold medallist at the 1934 International Six Days Trial and a member of the winning German Vase team in the 1935 ISDT. He also won the 1938 Bergmeister title in the German mountain-pass championship.

Besides his NSKK membership, Kluge was a fully-paid-up member of the Nazi Party too from May 1937 and was promoted within the NSKK from Obertruppführer to Stürmführer to acknowledge his political zeal.

Unsurprisingly, given his racing success and Nazi Party connections, Kluge was hailed as an Aryan superhero by the Nazi propaganda machine. He and his bike starred in a heroic bronze monument by the sculptor Max Esser installed in 1939 at the showpiece AVUS race track in Berlin (the main parallel straights of which survive as part of the Bundesautobahn 115 motorway). The other rider featured in this edifice was Ernst Henne, who had taken the world motorcycle speed record at 173.9mph on a BMW Kompressor in 1938.

Sissi Wünsche, another Dresdener born at Langebrück in 1916, was also on the Island for the third time. After scoring a sound fifth place in the 1937 Lightweight TT, his bike had seized on its first lap in 1938. His career had begun in 1933 as an 18-year-old DKW privateer with some creditable positions in mountain-pass races and on roads circuits. For the 1934 season, Wünsche acquired a 500cc AJS K10, which must have been four or five years old then. Despite its chain-driven overhead-camshaft engine, this proved notoriously unreliable so decent results eluded him. But the following year he went back to a 250cc DKW with some works assistance, taking four notable wins, and finally

got a full factory contract in 1937 for his TT debut.

Heiner Fleischmann, an easy-going Bavarian born at Amberg in 1914, was the younger brother of established German bike racer Toni Fleischmann who, along with future BMW star Otto Ley, had earned his spurs riding for the Triumph Werke Nurnberg (TWN) motorcycle manufacturing operation based in nearby Nuremberg. This company was originally an offshoot of the British Triumph concern in Coventry – which had been founded by a pair of Nurembergers, Siegfried Bettmann and Mauritz Schulte. TWN had become independent in 1929, producing a range of small two-stroke road bikes designed by Otto Reitz, who also developed 350cc and 500cc OHC four-stroke racing singles in the early 1930s.

Apart from his race contract, Toni Fleischmann was also employed at the TWN factory as an engineer and got his sibling a job there in the early 1930s, after the boy had finished his apprenticeship as a motor mechanic. Fleischmann Senior was subsequently head-hunted by NSU and took Heiner with him when he moved to Neckarsulm.

At NSU, Heiner Fleischmann soon began racing and immediately impressed both his brother and the management – with NSU supremo Baron von Falkenhayn taking an avuncular interest. His brother put together a well-prepped 350cc Bullus SS single for him and Fleischmann stormed the German national 350 championship with it, taking the title in 1936. He also paid his first visit to the Isle of Man that year as team-mate to Oskar Steinbach, using his 350 to gain a sound seventh place in the Junior TT – only 17 seconds behind Steinbach in sixth – but broke down in the Senior.

Fleischmann took the German 350 championship title again in 1937, so dominant that he won eight out of the ten rounds. But in 1938 he was obliged to introduce Moore and Röder's supercharged twin to the grid and suffered from its teething problems. Finishing as runner-up in the national series, he also couldn't help but notice the superior performance of his usurper Walfried Winkler's two-stroke DKW. So he jumped ship from NSU and signed up for the DKW factory in Zschopau for 1939. His return to the Isle of

Man TT that year was also the first round of a 350cc European championship campaign on behalf of his new benefactor at Zschopau.

There were also two British riders attached to the team. Ernie Thomas was in his third year with DKW for the 250cc Lightweight, having presumably been first recruited in 1937 as a veteran TT hand to show rookies Wünsche and Kluge the way round. He was actually their most successful entrant that year too, on the podium in third spot. A perhaps rather more unlikely addition for 1939 was the 30-year-old Scotsman Fergus Anderson, making his debut in the TT and beginning what would eventually prove to be an illustrious international racing career quite late in life. Anderson was entered in the Junior and the Senior on a 350. All three German team members were entered in the Junior and the Lightweight races.

The 250cc DKW Lightweight bike was basically the same rotary-valve supercharged split-single two-stroke that had been all-conquering in the hands of Kluge in 1938. Its secret was a pair of cylinders, one the combustion chamber and the other acting as a charging pump, incorporating Adolf Schnürle's patented loop-scavenge system with angled inlet ports. The 350cc machines for the Junior and Senior, appearing on the Island for the first time, were split-twins doubling up this configuration.

Local press comment, if not always accurate to the letter, was full of political hyperbole as the Nazi challenge materialised in the paddock. 'The DKW team, all well-acquainted with the TT course, will be Germany's Stormtroopers as far as the Junior is concerned,' warned the Isle of Man Weekly Times. And in its Lightweight forecast the same newspaper lumped hi-tech works entries from Fascist Italy's Benelli and Moto Guzzi factories in with the DKW enemy. 'The scrap for supremacy will almost certainly be between the Axis powers,' it said – even though, with the solitary exception of Omobono Tenni, all the Italian machines were being ridden by British competitors.

By comparison, the NSU team was an unknown quantity. Although well-established on home turf, its three

◆ Heiner Fleischmann first came to the Island for NSU in 1936 (facing page, left), the year he also won his first German 350cc championship on the same Bullus single. His 1939 DKW team-mate Ewald Kluge had just been honoured by inclusion in a bronze effigy, along with world speed record holder Ernst Henne, by sculptor Max Esser at the AVUS racetrack in Berlin (above).

German members – Karl Bodmer, Wilhelm Herz and Otto Rührschneck – had never been to the Island before. The one familiar British face they had on board was the inimitable John 'Crasher' White, who had undoubtedly been hired for his course experience. White's Isle of Man pedigree stretched right back to victory in the 1934 Manx Grand Prix Junior. And he had taken a total of seven top-five TT placings in the intervening four years, including three podium finishes.

Karl Bodmer was a native of Ebingen, south of Stuttgart, born in 1911. A motor mechanic by trade, Bodmer started racing in 1930 on a Victoria KR 50 S single – which had a British-made OHV 498cc Sturmey-Archer engine – and won the very first Alpine mountain event he entered. He became a works rider for the Victoria factory, which was located in Nuremberg, from 1931 to 1933. During this period he was a leading specialist over the mountain passes, also using a Victoria KR 35 fitted with a 350cc OHV JAP motor.

◆ NSU's 1939 Isle of Man TT squad was made up of Karl Bodmer, Otto Rührschneck and Wilhelm Herz (above, left to right). The British rider John 'Crasher' White was also set to use one of the factory's bikes in the Junior too. Apart from the fact that all three Germans were TT rookies, only having 350cc machines made their entries in the Senior as well as Junior rather optimistic. And the problems they'd already been experiencing with the bike on home turf would certainly be exacerbated by the very bumpy but extremely fast Mountain Course. On paper at least, this supercharged DOHC parallel twin looked promising but congenital overheating associated with the blower positioning made it very unreliable. It was also rather heavy, had only gestural suspension and handled badly. These detractions were a recipe for TT failure.

He latterly campaigned Imperia machines, made in Cologne and fitted with various proprietary engines, as well as Nortons and Triumphs.

Bodmer then earned a works DKW contract from 1934 to 1937, still up the sharp end over the mountains but also taking victory in many roads circuit events including the 1937 German Grand Prix, before moving to NSU for the 1938 season. Giving the new 350cc supercharged twin its baptism of fire alongside Heiner Fleischmann, he scored some good initial results, winning at the Hamburg Stadtpark in front of 80,000 spectators and also at the Schottenring. But, like Fleischmann, he also suffered from the machine's ongoing technical shortcomings and Bodmer failed to finish a lot of races that year.

Wilhelm Herz was yet another refugee from the DKW marque. Born in 1912 at Lampertheim just outside Mannheim on the Rhine, he was the eldest of eight children and was apprenticed as a carpenter in his father's business. But in 1930 he went to the Nürburgring to spectate at the

German Grand Prix and became utterly smitten. Two years later, having saved up to buy a 500cc DKW twin, he started club-level racing at the nearby newly-built Hockenheim track and won the 500 class in his first season. Then, after three years as a hobby-racing privateer and eventual qualification for an international competition licence, he became friendly with established star Oskar Steinbach – who also came from Mannheim – in 1935.

Steinbach was at that time riding for both DKW and NSU in various classes, and got the DKW factory's permission to lend Herz his spare works 500 for the 1936 Grand Prix of Europe at the Sachsenring. And this was followed up with the loan of a 350 NSU for the final Grand

◆ Ernie Thomas became a British mercenary for the DKW factory in 1937 and started that year's Lightweight TT as first man away on the road (top) in front of Stanley Woods – eventually finishing just under four minutes behind him in third place. Thomas stuck with DKW for the 1938 and 1939 events.

Prix round at Monza, where Herz finished an impressive fourth. A rising star, Wilhelm Herz had attracted the attention of the factories with these performances.

He initially tested for BMW at the Nürburgring at the end of 1936 but crashed the bike – resulting in an abrupt loss of Bavarian interest. However, he did get a firm offer from DKW to ride a works 500 alongside Oskar Steinbach in 1937 – and understandably jumped at the chance. Sadly, though, Steinbach was killed in a practice crash before the start of the season and the DKW squad for that year was Herz, Karl Bodmer and Karl Mansfeld.

Herz got off to a great start, with third place behind the factory BMW Kompressors in his first race at the Eilenriede track in Hanover. He then followed this up with a pair of fourths at the Solitudering and Sachsenring and got on the podium with third spot at the Grand Prix of Finland in Helsinki. But it was evident that DKW couldn't catch the Kompressors in the big-capacity league and also faced increasing competition from the likes of Gilera, Moto Guzzi and Norton. So at the end that season the factory decided to withdraw from the 500 class and Herz was out of a job.

He didn't give up, though, and managed to buy his pair of 1937-spec bikes from the DKW race department. Back as a privateer in 1938, he continued to get good results and finished up as fourth overall – and top privateer – in the 500 class of the German championship. Most notably, he won the Grand Prix of Europe at the Nürburgring. Once again his tenacity paid off and he was signed to ride for NSU in 1939 on the new blown twin that Fleischmann had apparently got competitive as runner-up in the 350 class of the 1938 national series. Like many of the other Germans, Herz came to the Isle of Man to begin a European championship bid.

The third member of the NSU team, Otto Rührschneck, is a bit of a dark horse historically with very little material charting his life and competition career. He was one of a pair of racing brothers. Most famously, Karl and Otto Rührschneck crossed the line at the Schottenring wheel-to-wheel in 1938 and were declared joint winners of an official dead heat – not something that happens these days since the advent of transponders and electronic timing.

In theory, Moore and Röder's new DOHC 346cc supercharged parallel twin – which these NSU team members were to use in both the Junior and the Senior – was a truly formidable confection. The striking appearance of its engine wouldn't have looked out of place decades later, apart from bevel drives to the overhead camshafts and reliance on long-since-banned forced induction. Revving to 8500rpm, it allegedly pumped out 45bhp – nearly as much power as the best 500cc Manx Norton or Velocette single of that period. But with a nine-gallon tank fitted to cope with fuel consumption of 12mpg around the Island, it weighed considerably more than 300lb despite magnesium crankcases.

Apart from excess weight, its problem was reliability and therefore performance over distance. This was essentially due to the positioning of the supercharger, tucked away on the gearbox casing behind the barrels, where it suffered from congenital overheating. Successful supercharged machines tended to feature blowers mounted in front of the motor to aid cooling. Handling wasn't too clever either, and the team was still experimenting with two different frames at the TT. Like the 1938 bikes, Herz, Rührschneck and White were using a rigid rear end with girder forks at the front. Bodmer's machine had plunger suspension grafted on at the back.

Set-up testing at Hockenheim before the TT expedition, presumably running typical Isle of Man Mountain Course race distances, had proved very disappointing – with poor lap times and incessant technical difficulties. It's probably fair to assume that the NSU contingent was somewhat subdued about its prospects upon arrival in the TT paddock.

◆ In his second year at NSU, Karl Bodmer (facing page) had cut his racing teeth on the big German mountain-pass hill-climbs before taking to the circuits with a DKW works ride from 1934 to 1937. Most notably he won the German Grand Prix for DKW in his final year with that factory. Obviously eager to tackle some of the new NSU twin's problems, Bodmer's TT bike benefited from plunger rear suspension rather than the rigid rear ends that his team-mates Wilhelm Herz and Otto Rührschneck were still lumbered with.

◆ The only man who could consistently beat the supercharged BMW 255 Kompressor twins was three-times European champion Jimmie Guthrie (above) – one of motorcycle racing's all-time greats. Guthrie consummately defeated the German challenge on his less-powerful and normally-aspirated Manx Norton single during the Kompressor's full season in 1936, with Karl Gall and Otto Ley playing second fiddle at almost every European championship round. And he was doing a fine job of keeping them at bay in 1937 too, until tragically killed at that year's German Grand Prix.

And finally we come to the BMW squad, who were focused entirely on winning the blue-riband Senior TT. Star of the show had to be Schorsch Meier, the reigning European 500cc champion, returning for his second hunt for victory on the Island. A Bavarian, Meier was born at Muldorf am Inn east of Munich in 1910. He joined the State Police when he was 19 years old, and then the Reichswehr military police. During a very successful career in off-road motorcycle sport – mentioned in chapter one – he turned in a spectacular performance at the final special high-speed test in the 1937 ISDT. Although most of this predominantly off-road event had been held in Wales, this test took place on tarmac at the new Donington Park race circuit in Leicestershire. Meier surprised everyone by winning it easily against British team members who were experienced road racers.

◆ Schorsch Meier came to the 1939 TT having won just about every single international event he'd entered the previous year apart from the TT. And although he later claimed never to have taken the Nazis seriously, Meier (above) certainly demonstrated no reluctance about joining in a 'Heil Hitler' routine with NSKK-Korpsführer Adolf Hühnlein when winning in Germany.

The BMW factory, which was looking for a replacement for veteran racer Otto Ley at that time and already supplied Meier with bikes, took due note of this performance. Meier was asked to try out a Kompressor during practice at a race meeting on the 7.6km Schleiz Triangle – the oldest roads circuit in Germany, first used in 1923. He reportedly came in after a few laps and complained that it was too dangerous but was persuaded to continue – and eventually posted the day's fourth-fastest practice time. And he got Ley's job for the 1938 season.

Apart from his ignominious demise for technical reasons at the start of the 1938 Senior TT on the Island, Meier rode a pure blinder for BMW during the rest of that year. In his debut race at Eilenriede, he took victory, lap and race records despite a start-line cock-up that put him last on the first lap. He then went on to win the Belgian Grand Prix at Spa-Francorchamps, the Dutch TT at Assen, the German Grand Prix at Sachsenring and the Italian Grand Prix at Monza – taking the European 500cc championship title by a big margin at his very first attempt. He also scooped the German 500 national championship.

In contrast to Meier, his German team-mate Karl Gall was at the end of a career that had been blighted by injury. Gall had put off his retirement from racing just to have one

last crack at the TT – particularly as everybody knew there wouldn't be another chance for some time because of the rapidly approaching war. And there has to be a suspicion that he must have pulled NSKK rank and Nazi Party influence to be included in the team at all. The previous year, he had been the slowest BMW rider through the practice speed trap at Sulby – and the only one running behind the factory Norton singles of Daniell, Frith and White. More obvious choices would have been Meier's main BMW-mounted sparring partner in the German and European championships for 1939, Ludwig 'Wiggerl' Kraus – or perhaps Otto Rührschneck's younger brother Karl, who was also a BMW factory rider in the German championship that year.

Gall, originally an Austrian, was born in Vienna in 1903 and automatically acquired German citizenship in March 1938 when Austria was annexed by the Nazis. He was the youngest of three motorcycle racing brothers – Franz, Adolf and Karl – and began competing in 1924. He first rode for the BMW factory in 1927 and 1928, mainly in long-distance off-road events and mountain-pass hill-climbs. The following year he got a works contract with Standard, a company based at Ludwigsburg north of Stuttgart, which manufactured motorcycles with MAG proprietary engines from the Swiss Motosacoche concern.

Gall returned to a BMW deal in 1930 but was so badly injured in a crash at the Nürburgring he was unable to race for the following three years – although he remained on the factory payroll as an engineer. Then, after a further two years riding for various other manufacturers, he again returned to BMW in 1936 to campaign the new 500cc Kompressor – which had been briefly showcased at the AVUS circuit in Berlin by Wiggerl Kraus in 1935 – alongside Otto Ley.

But neither he nor Ley could catch Jimmy Guthrie's Norton in the 500cc European championship for most of that season. Despite its superior power, the early Kompressor had a rigid rear end and its handling was dire. Ley managed a couple of second places behind Guthrie at the Swiss Grand Prix and Assen TT. Their best result was at the Swedish Grand Prix, which Ley won with Gall second after Guthrie broke down.

1937 was a different story and undoubtedly Gall's best year. The bike now benefited from plunger rear suspension designed by Alexander von Falkenhausen and a universal joint on the drive shaft to allow for wheel movement – so its handling was much improved. Gall and Ley were soon on the pace of the Nortons. Gall went on to win the Dutch TT at Assen and the German Grand Prix at the Sachsenring – after Guthrie was tragically killed on the final lap. Ley won the Swedish Grand Prix. Poignantly, Jimmy Guthrie nevertheless took a third successive European 500cc title, albeit posthumously. But a consolation for Karl Gall was victory in the German national championship's big-capacity class.

By comparison, 1938 was a complete disaster. Any hope of defending his German title or challenging for European laurels was snuffed out in what appears to have been a somewhat careless practice crash at the TT that June. Gall's season was over because he spent the rest of it languishing in a Manx hospital. So 1939 was his last chance for glory.

The trusty British TT regular 'Jock' John Milns West was also signed up once again in support of the two Germans. Born in the south-eastern outskirts of London at the leafy suburb of Belvedere near Erith in 1909 from parents of aggressively Scottish ancestry, West began riding motorcycles when he was 14 years old and entered his first race at Crystal Palace in 1927 on a 350cc Blackburne-engined Zenith. This debut was inauspicious, though, because he woke up back in the paddock on a stretcher after crashing.

But rather than being discouraged, West then went on to build a reputation for winning on the fast downland grass-track circuits of southern England, including Brands Hatch before it was surfaced. Supported with race machinery by his local Ariel dealer Walter Hartley in Plumstead, he soon attracted the attention of the Ariel factory. The result was the loan of a 500cc bike to attempt the 1931 Manx Grand Prix Senior race. But the crankshaft broke on his first lap. West returned to the Island for the following year's Manx with another Ariel and went well until his engine began to misfire badly on the last lap. He nevertheless finished 20th.

Graduating to the TT in 1933 with a three-year-old OHC 350 AJS for the Junior, he failed to finish thanks to a dropped inlet valve but caught the eye of quixotic Triumph supremo Edward Turner, who promised him a bike for 1934. Two torrid years riding for Triumph in the Senior TT ensued. In 1934, he fell off at Ballacraine, remounted and eventually retired at the end of his opening lap with a puncture. And then he failed to finish the Senior again in 1935. However, earlier that week, West scored his most promising result on the Island with a solid 15th place in the Junior on a considerably more useful works NSU Bullus 350, standing in for an injured factory rider. This was his first and decidedly positive experience of German motorcycles.

Having completed a five-year engineering apprenticeship with GEC at the end of 1935, he got a job with the small British sports car manufacturer Frazer Nash. This company had also just become official UK importer of BMW cars and bikes in knocked-down kit form and West was appointed sales manager responsible for the BMW motorcycles that the firm was assembling and marketing. So although he pushed a Vincent 500 into eighth spot after its chain broke on the last lap of the 1936 Senior TT, he was cheerfully blasting around on a shaft-drive BMW boxer demonstrator back in England – reportedly collecting a fine set of speeding tickets for Frazer Nash to pay.

West's new job led to direct contact with factory personnel in Germany and BMW motorcycle racing department manager Sepp Hopf got to hear of his TT exploits. Hopf invited him over for a test during early-season practice at the Eilenriede track, was duly impressed and then shipped a full-on 255 Kompressor to the Isle of Man with a mechanic, for West's assault on the 1937 TT. Riding as instructed for a finish, he nevertheless had to push in at the end to claim sixth place after running out of fuel.

This first attempt was good enough for the factory and, to show his appreciation, Hopf also supplied a bike for the Ulster Grand Prix later that year. Run on the Old Clady course near Strabane, which had a bumpy seven-mile straight, this event took place in heavy rain. West worked his way up through the field, hit the front and won – averaging 91.46mph over the 12 laps and 246-mile race distance.

His place in the BMW team for the 1938 TT was secure and he was the marque's only finisher after Gall and Meier's mishaps. He then went on to stand in for the injured Gall at the Belgian Grand Prix, coming third behind Meier and Freddie Frith, and capped a great year with another victory for BMW in the Ulster Grand Prix, breaking the outright lap record with 98.93mph and averaging 93.98mph for the whole distance. Inevitably, Jock West was included in BMW's plans for the 1939 TT.

By 1930s' standards, the BMW race team was a big-money outfit. Apart from factory director Christian Trotsch in charge, race department head Sepp Hopf as crew chief and a legion of factory technicians, it also had a physical training instructor – Herr Schuzler – in tow as well as dedicated medical support from its own surgeon, Dr Hans Bergermann. And there was nothing cheap about the equipment, either. In what would be its final year of international stardom, the BMW 255 Kompressor was unquestionably a significant landmark in motorcycling history.

Development had pushed power up almost to the 70bhp mark by 1939 – a huge advantage over competing British singles. Each cylinder of its 500cc boxer-twin motor had double overhead camshafts and bevel-drive timing gears but the real key to all this stomp was a Zoller multi-cell vane-type supercharger driven from the front of the crankshaft. And the advantages of the blower's positioning was that – unlike the ill-fated NSU twin – both the rotor casing and the resultant long intake tracts running underneath each cylinder were very effectively air-cooled, so it was reliable as well as extremely powerful.

The machine was also amazingly light – lighter than the British opposition – thanks to the widespread use of electron magnesium for crankcase and gearbox castings. And its handling had been steadily improved over the past three years with oil-damped suspension now at both ends – telescopic forks at the front and a plunger rear rig. It had also acquired much better brakes, in larger full-width hubs, the previous year.

In contrast, British resistance was somewhat subdued. The pre-eminent British motorcycle manufacturer Norton had stepped back from an earlier decision to pull out altogether because of military contract commitments but only supplied Harold Daniell, Freddie Frith and Crasher White with the same Senior machines they had ridden the previous year. Britain's best hope of saving its national pride in the Senior stakes was Velocette-mounted star Stanley Woods, because he came to the Island in 1939 armed with a secret new weapon.

Velocette had put together an ambitious challenger to German and Italian technological supremacy in the shape of its own 500cc supercharged twin – known as the 'Roarer' – which was to be unveiled at the TT. This radical pure racing machine had been conceived and manufactured from scratch in under a year. Charles Udall was credited with detailed design work under the direction of Velocette chief engineer Harold Willis.

◆ The BMW 255 Kompressor motor (above) was amazingly advanced for its day, with a power output of almost 70bhp by 1939. Star billing goes to a Zoller multi-cell vane-type supercharger, mounted on the front of the crank. Delivering 15psi of forced induction, its positioning and long inlet tracts also aided cooling - a vital factor given supercharged machines of the period tended to overheat. But it also had bevel-driven double overhead camshafts in each cylinder head and widespread use of electron magnesium for crankcase and gearbox castings ensured that it was significantly lighter than all of its competitors in the blue-riband 500cc class.

The engine layout was extraordinary. At a glance, it was a conventional four-stroke parallel twin configuration with side-by-side cylinders, although the exhaust ports faced backwards. But each piston and con-rod drove a separate crankshaft running fore-and-aft. These twin cranks were geared together with take-offs for the Centric supercharger – which ran at a fairly modest 4psi boost pressure – and a bevel drive to double overhead camshafts. The clutch and gearbox were on the back of one crank, leading to a universal joint and shaft final drive enclosed in the nearside strut of the swing arm. Velocette had been ahead of every other manufacturer with twin-shock swing-arm rear suspension on its bikes for more than a decade at that time.

The whole thing bristled with innovative engineering and state-of-the-art components. All the castings, apart from the barrels and cylinder head, were ultra-lightweight magnesium. The frame was a two-part structure that bolted together. The upper section could be removed with the headstock, front suspension and wheel still attached, leaving the engine easily accessible and still mounted in the lower half, complete with transmission, rear suspension and wheel.

But the trouble was that the first race Velocette had to win with the Roarer was getting it ready in time for the TT. And that was very much dependent on the energetic project direction of Velocette design supremo Harold Willis. Already a legend at the comparatively young age of 40, Willis had been a successful racer in his own right, with second places in the Junior TT in 1927 and 1928, but was equally well-known as a highly gifted development and design engineer. He had been responsible for the patented positive-stop foot gear change pioneered by Velocette in the late 1920s, was behind much of the success of the seminal K-series Velocette production racing bikes and was credited with a wide range of advances from the dual seat to swing-arm rear suspension, air suspension and even upside-down telescopic forks.

Tragically, a month before the TT, Velocette's race department was thrown into disarray when Willis was taken seriously ill and hospitalised with what later transpired to be meningitis – a life-threatening viral inflammation of the protective membranes surrounding the brain and spinal cord. The team left for the Isle of Man without him and were reportedly trying to assemble a complete bike – with a still-unpainted frame – on the ferry.

On the Island, attitudes towards the German invasion veered between bellicosity and appeasement. Probably the most acrimonious example of this was a pointedly jingoistic lead article penned by *Isle of Man Weekly Times* editor George Brown and the subsequent official response.

'Of course we don't want German or Italian riders to win and still less do we desire a victory for a British rider using a German or Italian machine,' opined Brown. 'Frankly, we deplore such happenings in a time like this. We are told that large sums of money are paid to these Englishmen. If Britons were riding these machines for sheer excitement, we should still consider them unpatriotic. There is more than a chance that the countries these famous British riders represent will be at war with Britain before the year is out.'

Brown then went on to attack Hitler and his cronies and call for much firmer Manx support for the UK government's rearmament efforts, including the introduction of military conscription on the Island – a subject on which Tynwald Court, the Isle of Man's parliament, was dragging its feet. And for prescient good measure, he added: 'We prefer not to speculate on TTs in 1940 and onwards.'

But on a freelance basis, separate from his regular newspaper commitments, George Brown had a contract to join the BBC radio race commentary team led by former TT star Graham Walker – father of more recent TV and radio motorsports mouthpiece Murray Walker – broadcasting from Creg-ny-Baa during the Lightweight and Senior events. His forthcoming on-air appearances had also been flagged up in the BBC publication *Radio Times*.

Four days after his editorial had hit the news stands, Brown got a phone call from Victor Smythe, the BBC producer responsible for TT coverage, informing him that his contract was cancelled with immediate effect. This was followed up the next morning by a letter from Mr J S Salt, the BBC's regional programme director.

'I noticed in the *Isle of Man Weekly Times* a leading article on the TT which raised certain questions in connections with the German entries,' wrote Salt. 'Since we had invited you to give the commentary from Creg-ny-Baa, it seemed possible that your published views on this aspect of the races might have to be taken into account. Accordingly, Mr Smythe reported to me this morning on the situation and after discussion here we felt that it would be most inadvisable at the present time for us to be associated with an element of political controversy in what we feel should be regarded purely as a sporting event. I therefore instructed Mr Smythe to inform you of our view and to make alternative arrangements for the commentary.'

So was this just the BBC scrupulously maintaining its reputation for objectivity? Not really. It had been bullied into ditching Brown. NSKK-Obergruppenführer Erwin Kraus had complained about Brown's opinions to his ACU counterpart, who referred the matter to the Isle of Man's Lieutenant-Governor Vice Admiral William Leveson-Gower – the senior UK government representative and most powerful man on the Island. It is likely that Leveson-Gower, who would succeed to the title of the 4th Earl Granville a month later and was married to the late Queen Mother's elder sister Rose Bowes-Lyon, simply had a 'word' with the BBC.

'The protest was lodged because we took exception to remarks about Herr Hitler,' DKW PR manager Karl Kudorfer (a Nazi Party member since 1923) told a reporter from UK popular newspaper *The Daily Sketch*. He went on to equate Brown's views to the 'yapping of a very small puppy' rather than the 'British Lion roaring'.

George Brown suspected that there was a cosier connection too, observing that Falkenhayn and other leading German factory representatives, Kraus, the BBC producer Smythe and a motley collection of ACU bigwigs were all staying at the same hotel and dined together – and had sat down to dinner at least once with His Excellency the Lieutenant-Governor. If Chamberlain in London had finally woken up to the looming Nazi threat, many people in the British establishment remained on cordial terms with them.

◆ Stanley Woods may well have been smiling when he brought the innovative Velocette Roarer supercharged twin out for a solitary practice lap with his Senior TT race number on it (facing page, left) but he wasn't happy with it. Billed as the only serious British challenger to Nazi technological supremacy, the Roarer just wasn't ready to race after its development had been disrupted by Velocette design guru Harold Willis falling ill a month before the TT.

◆ With all the respect for press freedom you'd anticipate from your average Nazi paramilitary thug, NSKK-Obergruppenführer Erwin Kraus (above) leaned on Isle of Man Lieutenant Governor Admiral William Leveson-Gower to arrange the dismissal of BBC radio TT race commentator George Brown, who had dared to be critical of the Nazis in a newspaper article.

◆ Shrugging off the previous year's mechanical misfortune and his Nazi team-mate Gall crashing out of contention in the opening 1939 practice session, Schorsch Meier (above) soon had plenty to smile about. On Monday of practice week he topped the Senior leaderboard with an 89.6mph lap and then did 90.27mph – the fastest performance in practice – the following day.

3 • PHONEY WAR

The BMW team arrived aboard the SS Fenella from Liverpool on the afternoon of 1 June 1939, and Schorsch Meier, Jock West and Karl Gall went out on their Kompressors in the following evening's practice. At the Highlander, Meier and West were seen riding in close formation 'with a noise like a couple of express trains'. At Bungalow it had become 'a shattering roar'.

Gall set off just four minutes after the session began 'to renew his acquaintance with the course', according to the *Isle of Man Examiner*. But he got no further than the humpback of Ballaugh Bridge, crashing on that opening lap and receiving what would prove to be fatal injuries. TT course marshals Sydney Shimmin, Robert Boyd and Charles Craine, along with Police Constable Stanley White, were witnesses to what transpired.

'Gall approached the bridge very fast on the left-hand side of the road and was attempting to pass another machine,' explained Shimmin at the subsequent inquest. 'Experienced riders all approach on the right-hand side so as to avoid the Glen Road wall after jumping the bridge. He realised the danger at the last moment, leaned his machine over to the left and came off.' Boyd described how Gall fell on the crown of the bridge and slid face downwards along the road for about 30 yards.

Craine and Constable White concurred with this, both agreeing that Gall had obviously taken the wrong line. 'I anticipated the crash,' Craine told the Coroner. 'He would have gone straight into the wall if he had continued, and he appeared to realise that.'

The policeman and one marshal carried Gall off the road while the others dealt with his bike. A local doctor was called to the scene by phone, arriving 15 minutes later. Upon seeing the horrific extent of Gall's injuries, he ordered him to be rushed to Ramsey Cottage Hospital by ambulance. When news of the accident reached the paddock, BMW team surgeon Hans Bergermann set off by car to Ramsey. Once there, he and resident surgeon Dr Robertson examined Gall and had his head X-rayed.

Jock West had ridden around the course on Meier's race bike at about 7.30pm, to find out what had happened. He telephoned the paddock from Ballaugh. 'Let Gall's friends know he is getting along nicely and resting,' he reportedly said in this call, presumably having been misled by people at the scene. He then returned to the Grandstand with Gall's helmet tied to his belt.

Gall wasn't 'getting along nicely', then or later. 'His condition was serious,' Bergermann reported to the Coroner. 'He was unconscious and had suffered a cerebral haemorrhage. There was a fracture at the base of the skull and a depressed fracture on the left side, a fractured nose and bleeding from the nose and mouth. The whole left side of the head and the nerve of the right eye were badly damaged.'

Bergermann immediately began an operation to tackle the depressed skull fracture and stop the haemorrhaging, assisted by Robertson and the hospital's Matron. Gall was deemed too ill to receive anything but a local anaesthetic. This operation was completed, apparently successfully, at 2am in the morning. For Robertson it must have been additionally stressful because he had attended Gall the year before. Doctor and patient had become friends during Gall's long convalescence and they had exchanged letters in the intervening months after he returned to Germany.

Gall's wife was flown to the Island to be at his bedside and Bergermann visited his patient several times each day,

later telling the Coroner that he had regained consciousness and steadily improved for a while. But, within a week, there were 'doubts as to his recovery' and another operation to relieve pressure on his brain was performed on Sunday 11 June. 'I examined him further to see if there were any signs of meningitis but there were none,' said Bergermann. 'However, I realised his condition had become critical.' Karl Gall developed pneumonia and died on Tuesday 13 June.

His coffin left the Island two days later, hitching a ride on the back of DKW's team truck the morning after the Lightweight race. The BMW and NSU squads were still preparing for the Senior in which he was to have ridden. The truck was met at the German frontier by a NSKK convoy accompanied by an honour guard of uniformed motorcycle outriders, to take him the rest of the way to Munich. Frau Gall had flown back in advance to supervise the funeral arrangements. Gall was subsequently interred with full Nazi paramilitary ceremonials at Munich's Waldfriedhof cemetery.

Practice and then racing carried on regardless. There was too much at stake to be sentimental about fallen comrades and a proposition that the BMW factory should withdraw Meier and West as a mark of respect was rejected out of hand. The only sign of contemplation was that the pair failed to make an appearance in morning practice on Saturday 3 June, the day after Gall's accident. But Meier and a number of other German contenders were seen indulging in illegal open-roads testing over the Mountain on Sunday. And on Monday he and West were officially back in action – and the fastest riders on the course with Meier heading the leaderboard courtesy of an 89.6mph lap.

Having arrived on Saturday afternoon aboard the Steam Packet vessel Mona's Queen, the NSU team with the factory's British designer Walter Moore as crew chief were also in action on Monday – but with considerably less encouraging results. Crasher White ground to a halt on his first lap with a seized motor at Ballagaraghyn. Leaving the bike, he walked to Ballacraine and managed to hitch a lift by car back to Douglas. Wilhelm Herz actually reached Ballacraine on his machine, but it died straight after the corner, the problem diagnosed as cooked spark plugs through overheating. He made several unsuccessful attempts to restart and then used the marshals' phone to call Race Control, before spectating for the rest of the session. Only Karl Bodmer and Otto Rührschneck managed to get all the way round – the former just once and the latter twice. But they were both well off the pace generally on lap times and about 15mph slower through the Hillberry speed trap than front-rankers like Freddie Frith, Ted Mellors and Stanley Woods on their Junior bikes.

The DKWs, meanwhile, were doing much better. And Heiner Fleischmann was going faster than Lightweight lap record holder Kluge. In that order the pair of them were the quickest 250cc riders through the speed trap. But, as a portent of things to come, the DOHC four-stroke Benelli of Ted Mellors was a second quicker than Fleischmann on their respective best laps and the other DKW team member Sissi Wünsche pushed Kluge off the top-three leaderboard by a 25-second margin.

The following morning, the die was effectively cast. In the Senior class, Meier was being noticeably aggressive and was seen to dive under and overtake his team-mate West going through Ballacraine on his opener, which from a standing start delivered an impressive 87mph result. Flashing straight past the Grandstand for a flying run, he then proceeded to get round in 25 minutes and five seconds at 90.27mph, only 12 secs slower than Harold Daniell's 90.99mph outright record established in 1938. This would prove to be the fastest of the year in practice. His third and final lap was much slower, simply because he stopped while approaching Ramsey to offer a pillion ride to Fleischmann, whose DKW had expired.

◆ For NSU's Wilhelm Herz (facing page, left) practice began as badly as it would continue throughout the week. On his very first attempted lap of the TT Mountain Course, he managed only slightly over seven miles – until his bike expired thanks to overheating at Ballacraine. His British team-mate Crasher White didn't even get that far, stopping at Ballagaraghyn with a seized motor. White managed to hitch a lift back to the Grandstand but Herz was stuck at the Ballacraine Hotel, spectating for the rest of the session.

◆ Practice week wasn't going according to plan for NSKK-Stürmführer Ewald Kluge (above) either. On the Tuesday of practice week, Benelli-mounted Ted Mellors got within two seconds of Kluge's 80.35mph outright Lightweight record set during his charge to victory in 1938, and comfortably topped the 250cc leaderboard. He would subsequently beat it by a much bigger margin.

Jock West, however, was eventually pushed into third place on Tuesday's Senior leaderboard by Velocette-mounted Stanley Woods who, although he was 37 seconds slower than Meier, in turn beat West by 23 seconds. Pointedly, though, he was on a single-cylinder machine and the supercharged Roarer twin was not in evidence. Herz went out with a Senior number on his 350cc NSU for a couple of laps but his best effort was a monumental nine minutes and 11 seconds off the front. Crudely translated into full race distance, he would be finishing more than an hour behind the winner on corrected time.

In the Junior stakes Woods was comfortably on top of a pile made up of Velocettes and Nortons, while the NSU factory's fortunes showed no sign of changing there either. Bodmer was best of the bunch, more than three minutes quicker than Herz (who was only entered in the Senior), followed by Rührschneck. White's troubles continued. He got as far as Ramsey where, according to witnesses, his bike 'gave a fireworks display' along Queen's Pier Road before stopping at the foot of May Hill. When he got it going again to tour in, he had to pick his way through a herd of sheep that had escaped onto the course below the Hairpin.

Putting the cat among German pigeons in the Lightweight, Mellors and his Benelli were also on the charge. His second lap took 28 minutes 13 seconds – 80.25mph – only two seconds slower than Kluge's 1938 outright record for the class. Fleischmann was a good leaderboard runner-up, 12 seconds in arrears of that, followed by Kluge and Wünsche. The latter had a big moment at Quarterbridge on his first lap, overshooting into Peel Road rather than taking the corner and then stopping at Braddan to adjust his brakes.

In another practice session that evening, Germans were the top performers in all three classes. Meier topped the Senior rankings with an 89.3mph lap, Wünsche led the Junior and Kluge was fastest among the Lightweight competitors. Glorious weather meant many riders – including Jock West – were complaining about melting tar on the roads. And NSU continued to suffer. Herz had a lucky escape when his engine seized while hammering flat-out down the Sulby straight,

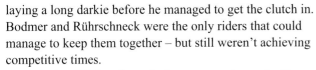

laying a long darkie before he managed to get the clutch in. Bodmer and Rührschneck were the only riders that could manage to keep them together – but still weren't achieving competitive times.

And on Wednesday a further menace to purely German rather than Axis hegemony in the Lightweight arrived, in the shape of Moto Guzzi co-founder and director Giorgio Parodi, and Guzzi's 1937 Lightweight victor Omobono Tenni, with supercharged 250cc four-stroke horizontal singles for Tenni and Stanley Woods to ride. These fuel-injected machines with Cozette blowers allegedly produced 38bhp at 7800rpm – more power than many 350 Junior bikes – and were capable of 130mph-plus.

'Signor Parodi has not been on the Island since Stanley Woods won the Senior for Guzzi in 1935,' noted the *Isle of Man Examiner*. 'In the intervening period he has been busy in Abyssinia with a war.' Italian Fascist troops had invaded and colonised Ethiopia – then called Abyssinia – in October 1935, using aerial bombing and poison gas against a local population generally armed with nothing more fearsome than the proverbial sharpened fruit. Parodi, who had been a fighter ace in the Italian Air Force during the First World War and was a keen Fascist advocate, took leave of absence from Moto Guzzi that year and volunteered to fight in Abyssinia

– collecting a medal from Mussolini for leading a bombing raid on the Abyssinian capital Addis Ababa.

Morning practice on Thursday saw uninterrupted BMW authority over the Senior leaderboard. Meier had remained fastest in every session, almost casually racking up repeated sub-26-minute laps. And West had grasped a firm hold on the runner-up spot with an 89.12mph run. Woods and Daniell held the Junior advantage, with Wünsche in third for DKW. But Moto Guzzi's potential in the Lightweight didn't become instantly apparent with Tenni breaking down at the Bungalow and Woods riding a leisurely sighting lap. Mellors' Benelli still held off the three DKWs, now in the order of Kluge, Fleischmann and Wünsche.

As for NSU, it was Bodmer's turn to fry his motor on the Sulby Straight. White's NSU 'didn't sound too healthy' at Braddan and then stopped for a while in Ramsey again. Only Rührschneck was making progress with a best time of 29 minutes and 24 seconds – the fastest NSU lap so far but still more than two minutes slower than Junior leader Woods.

◆ While Wilhelm Herz, Karl Bodmer and Otto Rührschneck (above left, left to right) were having a torrid time with their unreliable NSU machinery, they still managed to look happy posing for pictures in the paddock. DKW's Heiner Fleischmann (above right) was having a better time, close to Kluge in Lightweight practice and second behind Stanley Woods in the Junior stakes.

In the penultimate practice on Thursday evening, Germans led all three classes – Meier in the Senior, Fleischmann in the Junior and Kluge in the Lightweight – but the top of the leaderboards (Meier, Woods and Mellors) remained unchanged. However, Freddie Frith had usurped Woods for third spot in the Senior and Fleischmann had moved up to second in the Junior. But there were bigger surprises to come in the final practice on Saturday morning.

Fate had saved the worst until last for DKW. Guzzi star Omobono Tenni unofficially demolished the Lightweight outright lap record set by Kluge in the previous year's race by ten seconds – from a standing start. And then he did it again by a more resounding 38 seconds next time round. Tenni's tenure at the top was only temporary, though, because Ted Mellors was out there too. On his third circuit,

the Benelli rider punched in a time that was one minute and 43 seconds inside the record, translating into 85.54mph. This was even five seconds inside the outright Junior record! And the icing on Italian cake was that Woods on his Lightweight Guzzi went a second quicker than Kluge's best practice lap as well, to grab third place on the conclusive class leaderboard.

◆ When the Moto Guzzi team finally turned up late in practice week, Italian Fascist superhero Omobono Tenni and his supercharged and fuel-injected machine (facing page, left) – along with similarly-mounted Stanley Woods – ignominiously pushed the Nazi DKW triumvirate of Kluge, Fleischmann and Wünsche right off the Lightweight leaderboard. Although DKW's Sissi Wünsche (above) was the least competitive of the Zschopau factory squad and had suffered one or two embarrassing mishaps during practice, most notably overshooting the right-hander at Quarterbridge, he was still regarded as an experienced front-ranker in both the Lightweight and Junior.

◆ Making what would be his final Isle of Man TT appearance in 1939, ever-cheerful – and cheerfully mercenary – Irishman Stanley Woods (above) had a long and illustrious connection with the Moto Guzzi marque and team-mate Omobono Tenni. He first rode a Guzzi to fourth spot in the 1934 Lightweight TT. He then took Guzzi to both Senior and Lightweight TT victory in 1935, and broke down in the 1937 Lightweight – which Tenni won.

The week had not been without disappointments. Among British patriots a lot of hopes had been placed on the supercharged Velocette Roarer twin but it had been mysteriously absent. Basically, Stanley Woods had taken it out for a solitary run, realised that it was an under-developed turkey and elected to stick with his single-cylinder Senior Velocette. The man behind the Roarer, Harold Willis, still lay gravely ill in a Birmingham hospital. He never knew of its failure to deliver the goods, succumbing to meningitis on Monday 12 June at the beginning of race week. A bench dedicated to his memory stands just down the side of the Raven pub at Ballaugh Bridge. This was commissioned by colleagues at Velocette following his death and stood in the factory yard at Hall Green in Birmingham until the company closed down in 1971, after which it was moved to the Island.

There was also more controversy, mainly driven by widespread complaints about excessively noisy German race bikes with unsilenced exhausts illegally practicing on open roads as late as two o'clock in the morning. 'If motorcycles can make a row like that, what sort of hell on earth are we going to get from their guns?' observed one disgruntled local commentator.

NSKK-Obergruppenführer Kraus translated this remark in his post-TT report to Korpsführer Adolf Hühnlein. NSKK policy was to appear non-political at overseas events. Kraus and his stormtroopers never wore their paramilitary uniforms abroad – although NSKK insignia featured large on racing leathers – and he admonished BMW factory manager Christian Trotsch for undiplomatic bellicosity on the Island, by making 'a speech like the chairman of a war society'.

The noise issue was brought up in the Manx parliament Tynwald, where Members asked the presiding Lieutenant Governor to raise the matter with the Chief Constable. Other Members also took a dim view of the fact that the Isle of Man Government had paid travelling expenses to Britain for the German and Italian teams, and this was tantamount to subsidising the enemy. Lieutenant Governor Leveson-Gower rejected their criticism, claiming that all overseas competitors were treated equally.

Things came to a head when Police Sergeant Fred Faragher of the Isle of Man Constabulary, who was directing traffic at Governor's Bridge on the Sunday after the end of practice week, spotted DKW's Sissi Wünsche on his race machine being towed in by a mechanic on another motorcycle. Faragher told them that it was an offence to use an unlicenced and uninsured motorcycle except during official practice or racing and advised him to go straight back along Glencrutchery Road to the paddock. The two Germans apparently complied.

Just half an hour later, after the policeman had driven to Creg-ny-Baa, he saw Wünsche again – riding up towards the Mountain on the same machine. This time, he collared him. Wünsche was put before the High Bailiff and found guilty of riding a bike without licence, insurance, registration plate, horn and silencer. But mercy was shown by the court because the German couldn't speak English – and therefore potentially didn't have a clue what Faraghar was talking about – and he was fined only a total of one pound and ten shillings on three separate charges, with two shillings and eight pence costs. Some Manx wags were of the opinion that he should have been taken out and shot instead.

◆ The bench commemorating Velocette Roarer designer Harold Willis (top), which was originally located at the marque's factory in Birmingham, now stands down the side of the Raven pub in Ballaugh on the Isle of Man.

4 • BLITZKRIEG

Equating what happened during three TT races held on the Isle of Man in June 1939 with the spectacularly successful mechanised invasion of the Low Countries and France by the Wehrmacht and Waffen-SS almost exactly one year later is perhaps pushing the semantic envelope a metaphor too far. Certainly, the combined German attack at the beginning of race week didn't go according to any heroic battle plan.

THE JUNIOR

As the local *Isle of Man Examiner* newspaper had judiciously noted in its preview for the opening 350cc Junior TT, 'The NSU riders have not shown in practice that they will be a serious menace in the race'. The DKW squad, although presenting a greater fear, weren't right on top of their game either. More than just Irish eyes were smiling for Velocette-mounted Stanley Woods, who had been the fastest man in practice, was the previous year's winner, reigning holder of the Junior lap record at 85.3mph and already had nine TT victories under his belt. For betting men, Woods was odds-on favourite. The Nortons of Harold Daniell and Freddie Frith were also hot to trot.

Worse, Lightweight lap record holder and 1938 victor Ewald Kluge had completely failed to stamp his authority on the Lightweight practice leaderboard as expected. So DKW had pulled him out of the Junior at the last minute to concentrate on the 250cc event, leaving Heiner Fleischmann and Sissi Wünsche to fly the Zschopau factory's Swastika with Scottish TT rookie Angus Ferguson in support.

Some 61 bikes were wheeled out of the paddock to be warmed up, with Kluge among seven non-starters. All three NSU riders in contention – Karl Bodmer, Otto Rührschneck

and Crasher White – had just been fined for presenting their bikes for scrutineering late, suggesting frantic and increasingly desperate spannering activity in that section of the German camp.

Woods, carrying the number-one plate, was first away with a clear road ahead. But because of the start-number lottery in place at that period – rather than the modern system of moving faster riders in practice up the starting order – many of his nearest likely rivals were way down the field. This meant Woods would be well into his second lap before positions of all the leading players became apparent to spectators.

For instance, Frith carrying number six on his Norton started one minute and 40 seconds behind Woods and they were neck-and-neck at Ramsey with the same gap. Then he went on to pull 23 seconds out of Woods back at the Grandstand on the first lap after a quicker run over the Mountain. But Daniell, way down the queue on number 51, didn't actually push off the startline until Woods was at Ramsey. The unfairest aspect of this system is that top riders down the order had to try that much harder, brusquely shoving their way past numerous sluggards. Woods, starting far down the order in 1938, had apologised afterwards for the 'dirty riding' he'd utilised to get some usefully empty road in front of him.

◆ As a leaderboard stalwart with four TT podium finishes between 1935 and 1938, following victory in the 1934 Manx Grand Prix Junior, the mercenary services of John 'Crasher' White (facing page, left) for the 1939 Junior TT must have cost the NSU factory dear. However, an ongoing comedy of spectacular mechanical failures throughout practice and the race must have been fairly humiliating for this deeply competitive rider. Fifth place in the Senior, safely back on a less radical but more reliable Manx Norton, helped to save his face.

First German away was DKW-mounted Wünsche on number eight, followed by his team-mate Fleischmann on 21 some four minutes later. Bodmer led the NSU trio off on number 28, followed by White on 36 and Rührschneck on 43. Ferguson, right down the order on 67, was the last of the DKWs away from the Grandstand – and second last overall, with only Harvey Deschamps on a Norton as tail-end charlie.

The weather had been fine at the start, after earlier showers, but reports came back of rain at Ramsey and then at the Bungalow. Commentators around the course were also reporting the attrition rate. A couple of riders had bitten the dust at Quarterbridge and another had 'a discussion with the hedge' at Creg-ny-Baa. White was also having a torrid time with his NSU. He had stopped at Kirk Michael to 'make adjustments' but eventually got going again – only to retire back at the Grandstand, quoting 'plug trouble'.

When all the leaders had finally finished that opening lap, the bets on Woods had begun to look misplaced - and the Nazi challenge had emerged. Frith was in front but Fleischmann was only 15 seconds behind him with Daniell another two seconds adrift. Woods was a further six seconds in arrears. Les Archer – the 'Aldershot Flyer' – and Ted Mellors on two more Velocettes were fifth and sixth with Wünsche's DKW in seventh place.

Up at the sharp end on the second circuit, Frith held the lead from Fleischmann but the German had eaten a second out of the Englishman's advantage and Woods was only a further seven seconds behind. Daniell had fallen off in Ramsey's Parliament Square and then restarted, losing two places in the process. Mellors was now fourth and Archer sixth. A hard-charging Sissi Wünsche was only a second back from them in seventh. There was blood on the track too, after the coming-together of Danish rider Sven Sorensen and H B Waddington at the bottom of Bray Hill. The latter was rushed to Noble's Hospital in Douglas with serious head injuries. And another of the ill-starred NSUs had expired, as Otto Rührschneck pulled into the pits with a fried clutch.

The last NSU gave up the ghost over the Mountain on the third lap when Karl Bodmer's machine overheated and seized. As far as the Germans were concerned, the honour of the Third Reich now rested solely on DKW shoulders. Both Frith and Woods made impressively fast fuel stops at the beginning of that lap but Fleischmann's sojourn in the pit lane was longer. As a result he dropped back to third place – but the three of them were still only separated by 25 seconds. Daniell, meanwhile had reacted to his embarrassment in Ramsey on the previous lap and taken fourth spot from Mellors, 36 seconds behind the German.

The leading pair of Nortons fared less well on lap four, though. Woods wound up his Velocette to get in front of Frith by two seconds while Daniell dropped back to fifth behind Mellors on the other Velocette. Fleischmann maintained third and Wünsche seventh. Woods was now really on song and put in the fastest lap of the race up to that point – 84.66mph – on his fifth circuit, not realising that his advantage over Frith had become infinite. The latter had parked his bike at Ballaugh with a sick engine. However, this didn't benefit Fleischmann because Daniell had woken up again and passed both Mellors and him. For DKW the only consolation was that Wünsche had moved up into sixth.

They all pitted again for fuel and Woods began lap six ahead on the road and leading the race by 32 seconds. But Daniell certainly hadn't settled for runner-up status yet, claiming the fastest lap so far with an 84.98mph average, cutting the gap further to 23 seconds. Fleischmann soldiered on in third, another slow refuelling ensuring that he was now adrift by one minute and 26 seconds. Wünsche had suffered the same fate in the pit lane, allowing yet another Velocette ridden by David Whitworth to rob him of sixth place.

Starting his final flying lap, Woods probably thought he had it in the bag. But after finishing he had a long wait until Daniell came home before victory was confirmed. And then

◆ Karl Bodmer (facing page, left) earned the dubious honour of being star performer on NSU's supercharged twin in the Junior. After his team-mates White and Rührschneck retired with mechanical woes on laps one and two respectively, at least Bodmer got most of the way round a third circuit before his steed expired for broadly similar reasons on the Mountain.

it was only by eight seconds. Daniell had put in the fastest lap of the race at 85.05mph – only five seconds outside the Junior outright record. This impressive charge was almost matched by Heiner Fleischmann, who lost just a single second against him over the last circuit to firmly hold third step on the podium. Wünsche regained sixth at the end thanks to Archer's ill-luck, running out of petrol and pushing in to take a lowly 24th place. As for Angus Ferguson on the third DKW, his performance during the race and retirement at some point went unremarked by contemporary commentators.

Two leading British marques had beaten the Reich. And a supremely lacklustre NSU input, with the factory's entire entry failing to finish, must have considerably increased displeasure among the Germans. Walter Moore was probably avoiding eye contact with Baron von Falkenhayn after that.

THE LIGHTWEIGHT

After a hardly earth-shattering third in the Junior, Germany was undoubtedly looking for redemption from DKW in Wednesday's Lightweight, with NSKK-Obertruppführer Ewald Kluge originally expected to lead Fleischmann and Wünsche - with Ernie Thomas in support – to domination. But DKW had been completely cast into the shade by Italian surprises at the end of practice week. The mood on that morning was sombre, not least due to news of Karl Gall's death on the previous afternoon, and so was the weather. Heavy cloud hung over the Island and reports of rain at Ballacraine and poor visibility elsewhere started to come in as bikes were warmed up and brought to the line. With 31 entries including five non-starters, the start schedule was less hectic than in the Junior, so there were 30-second intervals between riders.

The Benelli of Ted Mellors went away first on the road, followed shortly afterwards by Omobono Tenni on his Guzzi. Siegfried Wünsche, with the number-six plate was a minute and a half behind him. Ernie Thomas's DKW carried number 14 but was 12th to go because of non-starters. Heinrich

Fleischmann set off on number 18. Stanley Woods on the other trick Guzzi was right back at number 26, with DKW's brightest hope Ewald Kluge having drawn the shortest straw on 29 – third from last off the grid.

Mellors reached Kirk Michael in ten minutes but by then Tenni was only 14 seconds behind him. Fleischmann had already dropped 30 seconds on Mellors by the time he'd got to Ballacraine. Stanley Woods had also pulled out nearly half a minute against Kluge at Kirk Michael. And Ernie Thomas had stopped to change a plug at Ballacraine. It looked like a set-piece battle between to the two Italian marques, with Moto Guzzi in the ascendant – particularly because Tenni had caught Mellors on the road at Ramsey and Wünsche was also in trouble at nearby Crossags, stopping to 'make adjustments'.

But the weather was deteriorating fast and marshals at Creg-ny-Baa reported that they couldn't see Kate's Cottage due to fog. Visibility was actually down to 25 yards in places over the Mountain. Tenni nevertheless kept on pressing hard, a second ahead of Mellors at the Creg on the road and 15 seconds in front of him back at the Grandstand – a 45-second advantage on corrected time. But Woods on the other Guzzi was also on the charge and finished that first lap 37 seconds in front of the Benelli as well. German honour was down to Kluge, another 54 seconds adrift in fourth and Fleischmann trailing a further 20 seconds in fifth. Wünsche was seventh.

But Guzzi's star began to fade on the second lap. Mellors got to Ramsey nearly two minutes before Tenni – who was afflicted with gearbox misbehaviour – and Woods was in trouble too, dropping right off the leaderboard at Kirk Michael. When they came in for fuel, Mellors was leading by 31 seconds from Tenni and Kluge was only 28 seconds

◆ If Heiner Fleischmann (facing page, left) only looked moderately pleased with his third place podium in the Junior and the redemption of an absolute flyer on his final lap, amply-girthed DKW race director Adolf Meurer seemed effusive enough in the congratulations department. The other smartly-dressed gentleman sporting a similar felt hat stood directly behind Fleischmann – and untypically smiling – is none other than NSKK-Obergruppenführer Erwin Kraus, carefully incognito in civvies rather than his preferred jackboots.

behind him in third. But Fleischmann was suffering problems and had fallen back, letting the Excelsior-mounted Irishman Henry Tyrell-Smith up to fourth. Wünsche, though, had moved up to sixth and was hanging on in there. By then the weather was atrocious – with lashing rain most of the way round the course and dense fog across the Mountain.

Attrition bit heavily into the field on lap three. Tenni stopped twice before parking up and retiring from the race at Ballaugh. And numerous other riders were reported missing, presumed retired. Among them was Heiner Fleischmann, who had vanished – reportedly between Kirk Michael and Ballaugh. A travelling marshal was despatched to look for him on that section, without result. However, Woods appeared to have kicked some life into his Guzzi again and made it back up into fourth spot behind Tyrell-Smith. Wünsche had slipped to seventh. Fleischmann was eventually found, walking into Sulby.

On the fourth lap, Woods was in the ascendant, catching and pulling out a 38-second advantage over Tyrell-Smith. But he was more than a minute behind Kluge who, in turn, trailed Mellors by more than two minutes. It wasn't to last. The second of the Guzzis died at Crosby on lap five, putting Woods out, and Mellors continued to stretch his lead over Kluge to more than three minutes. In what were described as 'the worst weather conditions imaginable' retirements came thick and fast, and the closing stages saw the order unchanged apart from Wünsche moving up to fifth.

At the conclusion of the race, Ted Mellors took victory for Benelli in the slowest Lightweight for four years, beating Ewald Kluge definitively by three minutes and 45 seconds. Henry Tyrell-Smith completed the podium. Siegfried Wünsche was fifth and Ernie Thomas eighth for DKW, among only 13 finishers. The Reich had taken two podiums so far, but no top step. Hitler's master race was clearly malfunctioning.

Before Friday's Senior, there was another headline event – the official unveiling of the Guthrie Memorial on the evening of Thursday 15 June. Scots-born Jimmie Guthrie – one of Britain's all-time-greatest motorcycle racers and a

◆ NSKK-Stürmführer Ewald Kluge (facing page, left) was a very lucky Nazi in the Lightweight because – as in practice – he'd been firmly evicted from podium placing in the early stages of the race by Benelli-mounted Ted Mellors and the two Guzzis of Omobono Tenni and Stanley Woods, all of whom comprehensively cleared off. But mechanical failures by the latter pair eventually rewarded the German with his runner-up accolade. Appalling weather conditions were a major factor in culling the field – including DKW teamster Heiner Fleischmann – and only 13 contestants took the chequered flag. One of those who battled on to the end through rain and fog was DKW's Sissi Wünsche (above). After dropping back to seventh at one point, retirements by other riders finally gifted him fifth spot.

◆ In the capable hands of Ted Mellors (above), Benelli's DOHC single earned a resounding Lightweight victory for Fascist Italy over its fellow Axis power. But Ewald Kluge and DKW retained the outright lap record for the class. Appalling weather conditions throughout the race precluded the possibility of Mellors being able to repeat his sensational performance in practice, when he'd beaten Kluge's record by a large – albeit unofficial – margin.

winner of six TT races during his career – had been fatally injured while leading the last lap of the German Grand Prix at the Sachsenring in August 1937. That connection provided an excellent excuse for Nazi paramilitary strutting, which was amply exploited as Germans turned out in force for the ceremony.

The Memorial, a stone cairn located up on the Mountain between the 26th and 27th milestones, at the point where Guthrie retired in his final TT two years earlier, had been paid for through a public subscription orchestrated by Geoffrey Smith - managing editor of *The Motor Cycle* (the leading UK motorcycling publication of its day). His Excellency the Lieutenant-Governor Vice Admiral Leveson-Gower did the honours, drawing aside a Union Flag to reveal an inscribed plaque hailing Guthrie. Sergeant-Major Repton and Sergeant Baker of the 15th (Isle of Man) Anti-Aircraft Regiment played 'The Last Post' on bugles.

And then, right on cue, up stepped Baron von Falkenhayn and NSKK-Obergruppenführer Erwin Kraus to lay a lavish black wreath decorated with the Swastika emblem on a red sash. The pair of them stood to attention and their arms went up in the 'Heil Hitler' salute – echoed by a disciplined rank of German riders. The Baron concluded with a short speech in German, which he repeated in English. The large crowd of spectators remained silent.

Although the cause of Guthrie's death remained inconclusive and was never thoroughly investigated, more than half a century later Stanley Woods made a disturbing allegation of German involvement. 'I am prepared to go on oath that Guthrie was fouled,' claimed Woods in a 1992 interview shortly before his own death. 'I saw the accident because I was coasting to a halt with a broken petrol pipe. Two riders passed me, a German and Guthrie. It was just before a downhill right-hander which Jimmie took flat out. The German knew Guthrie was right behind him, for he'd

◆ Located at a point on the TT Mountain Course previously known as The Cutting, Guthrie's Memorial (left) has successfully withstood the elements for 70 years since it was unveiled in somewhat controversial circumstances.

◆ As utterly dominant in the Senior race as he had been in practice, Reichswehr Feldwebel Schorsh Meier hit the front with a 90.33mph opening lap from a standing start and then went through on 90.75mph for his second circuit, only a tad over four seconds outside Daniell's outright TT record set the previous year. BMW's 'modern Nazi product' was delivering the goods for Hitler.

been there for some time. But the German couldn't take it flat out, slackened and pulled into Jimmie's path, forcing him off the road into a line of saplings.'

At that point in the race, BMW works riders Karl Gall and Otto Ley were lying second and third behind Guthrie's Norton, and weren't involved in the accident. The German back-marker about to be lapped was allegedly DKW factory rider Karl Mansfeld. Woods was the first person to reach Guthrie, who ended up in a ditch.

'I could see he was in a desperately bad way,' recalled Woods. 'Both legs and an arm were broken but he had no head injuries. I don't think he knew he was dying. I went in the ambulance with him to the hospital but the roads were choked and it took two hours. After 20 minutes or so the surgeon came out and said that they'd revived him momentarily but that he had died. You can imagine how I felt. We'd been friends, team-mates and rivals for ten years. I was shattered.'

To be fair, though, the responsibility for Jimmie Guthrie's death almost certainly lies with the lengthy delay in treatment of serious injuries that would have seen him sinking into deep shock in the back of that ambulance. And one has to ask why Woods waited for so long before revealing this version of events.

THE SENIOR

Friday's blue-riband Senior race was the Germans' last chance for glory. But with Schorsch Meier odds-on favourite for BMW after his stellar performance in practice week, and Jock West supporting with a solid second spot on the leaderboard, they had to be confident. The weather had been transformed too. Conditions were dry and sunny with only a light breeze.

With 47 starters and seven rated contenders spread right through the field – thanks again to the race-number lottery – it was going to be a difficult call during the first lap. The previous year's winner and outright lap record holder Harold Daniell was first away on the road for Norton. But

as riders started at 20-second intervals, Stanley Woods on a factory Velocette wasn't flagged away until two minutes and 40 seconds later. Two minutes passed before the second Norton star, Freddie Frith, got off the line. Then the gap to Ted Mellors – on the other works Velocette – was three minutes and 40 seconds. The BMW challenge began after a further two minutes with Jock West. Meier, stuck with a late 49 plate, followed after a further four minutes and 40 seconds. The last of the best and penultimate starter, Crasher White on a third factory-spec Norton, got away 40 seconds behind Meier.

Daniell's title defence unravelled rapidly. Back at the Grandstand he had not only been passed by David Whitworth – who had started directly behind him – but also by Woods, with an advantage of more than three minutes. Frith came through three seconds shy of Woods' time. Mellors was a lot slower, adrift by 53 seconds, but West exactly matched Woods so they were neck-to-neck on corrected time. Then Meier thundered across the line to complete a 90.33mph lap from a standing start – a commanding 52 seconds faster than Woods and West. White slotted into the pack in front of Mellors in fifth spot when he finally arrived.

Four more riders were out there representing the Reich to a greater or lesser degree – three NSUs in the hands of Bodmer, Herz and Rührschneck, and Anderson on a lone DKW left behind by the already-departed factory team. But all of these were 350cc machines never likely to be in contention.

On lap two, Frith had pulled back an advantage over Woods at Ramsey but squandered it over the Mountain, finishing 15 seconds adrift. West, meanwhile, was on a charge and had pulled out five seconds on the Irishman. And then Meier went even faster, punching in a 90.75mph lap only slightly over four seconds short of the outright record. White held onto fifth, 33 seconds ahead of Mellors. Less impressive was the first of the also-ran NSU entries to destroy its engine, forcing the retirement of Wilhelm Herz.

As some riders began to come in for fuel at the end of lap three, Woods was now 15 seconds behind West but had

stretched his lead over Frith's Norton to a more comfortable 36 seconds. But he then threw it all away after filling his tank. Pushing off from the pits along the Glencrutchery Road, more than half a minute passed before his engine fired. As that gap shrivelled to nothing, another was getting bigger because Meier had matched his opening 90.33mph lap and was off the front by one minute and 35 seconds. A swift 28-second pause for petrol and clean goggles only served to increase his edge over the opposition. But bad news for the Nazis was that Rührschneck had blown up yet another NSU motor on the Sulby straight.

For Woods, his difficulties in getting the bike to fire up after refuelling had cost Velocette third place at the end of the fourth lap. But Frith was only 18 seconds ahead. West had apparently closed the gap on Meier at the front to one minute and eight seconds, because he had yet to make a fuel stop. Daniell, who had been gradually drifting back through the field with a sick clutch, finally retired at the Gooseneck. Mellors had also fallen off the pace so Velocette-mounted Les Archer moved up to sixth behind White. And the last chapter of NSU's jinx was Bodmer out of fuel and out of the race at Ramsey.

One contemporary news report noted that Meier had overtaken 26 other riders on the road at this point in proceedings. Another rather sniffily opined that 'it looked as if the modern Nazi product was going to outclass

last year's Norton'. And as if to underline that sentiment, Meier was fastest man again on his fifth circuit, extending his lead over West to more than two minutes. He, in turn, was now one minute and five seconds ahead of Woods – who had regained third place from Frith by 22 seconds. White and Archer held station, with Mellors recovering to seventh place. Anderson's lonely DKW was reported to have lost its exhaust pipe.

Into their sixth circuit, the gap between the two leading BMWs narrowed marginally to just two minutes after Meier pitted for fuel for the last time. A belated British counter-attack had begun, however, with Woods closing to 58 seconds behind West and – more impressively – Frith trailing him by only 16 seconds. But it was a case of too little and too late.

Jock West had stopped for a splash of fuel at the beginning of his seventh and final lap, allowing Schorsch Meier to take the chequered flag by a margin of two minutes and 20 seconds.

Later insinuations that West had been 'riding to orders' – thereby gifting victory to Meier – were based on that final pit stop, which he probably hadn't needed to make. But they don't stand up to close analysis. The fragile reliability of racing motorcycles 70 years ago and the particularly arduous nature of the 37.73-mile TT course made such sophistry a risky exercise – because the chances of any team member suffering a mechanical failure or

◆ Jock West (facing page, left), seen here going into Governor's Bridge on the other factory BMW Kompressor, was also riding a blinder. From lap two onwards, he stamped his name firmly on runner-up spot – but was never in contention for the win.

◆ Fortunately for subsequent generations of TT victors, the Nazis were not allowed to go home with the Senior trophy (left), originally donated by the Marquis de Mouzilly St Mars. If a takeaway had been countenanced, it's unlikely that we would have ever seen it again.

mishap were unpredictably high. A judicious team approach to guaranteeing victory was therefore every man for himself.

Furthermore, the technicalities of managing 'team orders', if they were indeed proposed, would have been beyond practicality. With the rudimentary communications and signalling procedures of the time, and the fact that West was running some distance ahead of Meier on the road throughout the race owing to his much lower race number, any attempt would almost certainly have ended in chaos or farce. And besides that, West never actually matched Meier's stupendous pace in either practice or race. It cannot be denied that Cast Iron Schorsch was the best man on the day.

Although the German's fastest lap had been fractionally short of the outright record, his 89.38mph average for the whole seven laps had beaten Daniell's 89.11mph race record from the previous year. And BMW had successfully scored the sort of supremacy the Nazis needed with a one-two knockout. But third didn't go to Stanley Woods. Frith pipped him at the post by 12 seconds – which meant he'd spirited up 28 seconds from somewhere on the last lap. Anderson's dilapidated DKW managed to limp home in 28th place out of 30 finishers.

The ensuing winners' enclosure spectacle was unprecedented for what the mealy-mouthed BBC had insisted was a purely sporting rather than political event. Team management and mechanics fell in alongside Meier and their right hands went up in unison for the Nazi 'Heil Hitler' salute. A sporting gesture? Jock West stood next to Meier, looking bemused and fiddling with his gloves. The Führer most emphatically had his propaganda coup.

◆ After the Nazis had got their synchronised 'Heil Hitler' saluting routine in the winners' enclosure out of the way, Schorsch Meier and Jock West (facing page left, left to right) looked understandably pleased with the team's effort. And although Meier had failed to snatch the outright lap record from Harold Daniell, he did achieve the fastest-ever average race speed to date for his seven laps of the Mountain Course with 89.38mph. This stood until 1950, when Geoff Duke led a group of five faster men over the line in that year's Senior.

JUNIOR ENTRIES

NO	NAME	NATIONALITY	MACHINE
1	S Woods	Irish	348cc Velocette
2	C F Brett	British	348cc Velocette
3	A R Foster	British	346cc AJS
4	F Vaasen	German	348cc Norton
5	G G Murdoch	British	348cc Norton
6	F L Frith	British	349cc Norton
7	G H Hayden	British	348cc Velocette
8	S Wünsche	German	346cc DKW
9	W H Craine	British	348cc Norton
10	K R H Rose	British	348cc Velocette
11	R Loyer	French	348cc Velocette
12	J Lockett	British	348cc Norton
14	L A Dear	British	348cc Velocette
15	F J Mussett	Australian	348cc Velocette
16	G E Rowley	British	346cc AJS
17	W Bold	British	348cc Norton
18	G Newman	British	348cc Velocette
19	J C Galway	S African	349cc Norton
20	E A Mellors	British	348cc Velocette
21	H Fleischmann	German	346cc DKW
22	H B Caldwell	British	348cc Velocette
23	Y Cauchy	French	348cc Velocette
24	E S Oliver	British	348cc Velocette
25	W R Lunne	British	348cc Velocette
26	S M Miller	British	348cc Velocette
27	N B Pope	British	348cc Velocette
28	K Bodmer	German	346cc NSU
29	S A Sorensen	Danish	349cc Excelsior
30	H G Tyrell-Smith	Irish	349cc Excelsior
31	M Cann	British	348cc Norton
32	L Cora	French	348cc Velocette
33	W T Tiffen	British	348cc Velocette
34	H B Waddington	British	348cc Norton
35	L V Perry	N Zealander	348cc Velocette
36	J H White	British	346cc NSU

JUNIOR ENTRIES CONTINUED

NO	NAME	NATIONALITY	MACHINE
37	F J Binder	Dutch	348cc Velocette
38	S Wood	British	348cc Velocette
39	M D Whitworth	British	348cc Velocette
40	J Williams	British	348cc Norton
41	J Garnett	British	348cc Velocette
42	G H Briggs	British	348cc Norton
43	O Rührschneck	German	346cc NSU
44	C H Manders	British	349cc Excelsior
45	F W Fry	British	348cc Velocette
46	L G Martin	British	348cc Norton
47	J W Beevers	British	348cc Velocette
48	E Kluge	German	346cc DKW
49	H B Myers	British	348cc Velocette
50	W F Rusk	British	348cc Velocette
51	H L Daniell	British	349cc Norton
52	H Pinnington	British	346cc AJS
53	J E Little	British	348cc Velocette
54	J M West	British	348cc Velocette
55	R Gibson	British	348cc Velocette
56	N Croft	British	348cc Norton
57	C Redfearn	British	348cc Velocette
58	L J Archer	British	348cc Velocette
59	H C Lamacraft	British	348cc Velocette
60	A K Millington	British	348cc Norton
61	N Christmas	British	348cc Norton
62	E R Thomas	British	348cc Velocette
63	L B Cherriman	British	348cc Norton
64	M Simo	Spanish	350cc Terrot
65	E S Cullingham	British	346cc AJS
66	L R Higgins	British	348cc Velocette
67	F Anderson	British	346cc DKW
68	H P Deschamps	British	348cc Norton
69	G V Dickwell	Belgian	246cc Benelli

JUNIOR FINISHERS

POS	NAME	MACHINE	TIME	AV SPEED
1	S Woods	Velocette	3.10.30.0	83.19
2	H L Daniell	Norton	3:10.38.0	83.13
3	H Fleischmann	DKW	3:12.05.0	82.51
4	E A Mellors	Velocette	3:12.28.0	82.34
5	M D Whitworth	Velocette	3:19.09.0	79.58
6	S Wünsche	DKW	3:20.57.0	78.87
7	M Cann	Norton	3:21.10.0	78.78
8	S Wood	Velocette	3:21.45.0	78.55
9	J E Little	Velocette	3:22.36.0	78.22
10	F J Mussett	Velocette	3:24.14.0	77.6
11	L G Martin	Norton	3:26.08.0	76.88
12	G H Hayden	Velocette	3:26.15.0	76.84
13	H G Tyrell-Smith	Excelsior	3:26.23.0	76.79
14	N B Pope	Velocette	3:26.42.0	76.66
15	W T Tiffen	Velocette	3:26.48.0	76.64
16	J Lockett	Norton	3:27.17.0	76.46
17	E S Oliver	Velocette	3:27.53.0	76.24
18	L A Dear	Velocette	3:28.15.0	76.1
19	H C Lamacraft	Velocette	3:28.33.0	75.99
20	W F Rusk	Velocette	3:28.53.0	75.87
21	G Newman	Velocette	3:29.03.0	75.81
22	F J Binder	Velocette	3:29.09.0	75.77
23	G E Rowley	AJS	3:29.54.0	75.5
24	L J Archer	Velocette	3:29.55.0	75.5
25	C F Brett	Velocette	3:30.18.0	75.36
26	J C Galway	Norton	3:31.40.0	75.23
27	J W Beevers	Velocette	3:34.44.0	73.8
28	S M Miller	Velocette	3:35.46.0	73.45
29	L R Higgins	Velocette	3:35.57.0	73.39
30	J M West	Velocette	3:36.41.0	73.14
31	J Garnett	Velocette	3:28.37.0	72.55
32	H B Caldwell	Velocette	3:39.56.0	72.06
33	R Gibson	Velocette	3:40.54.0	71.74
34	G H Briggs	Norton	3:43.34.0	70.89
35	H B Myers	Velocette	3:50.28.0	68.77

LIGHTWEIGHT ENTRIES

NO	NAME	NATIONALITY	MACHINE
1	E A Mellors	British	246cc Benelli
2	O Tenni	Italian	249cc Moto Guzzi
3	H C Lamacraft	British	249cc Excelsior
4	W H S Pike	British	249cc Rudge
5	J M West	British	246cc New Imperial
6	S Wünsche	German	248cc DKW
7	H G Tyrell-Smith	Irish	249cc Excelsior
8	M Simo	Spanish	250cc Terrot
9	J Williams	British	246cc New Imperial
10	S A Sorensen	Danish	249cc Excelsior
11	R L Graham	British	249cc CTS
12	C H Manders	British	249cc Excelsior
14	E R Thomas	British	248cc DKW
15	J McCredie	British	249cc Excelsior
16	L G Martin	British	249cc Excelsior
17	C B Taylor	British	247cc CBT
18	H Fleischmann	German	248cc DKW
19	L J Archer	British	246cc New Imperial
20	S Wood	British	249cc Rudge
21	H Hartley	British	249cc Rudge
22	C Tattersall	British	249cc CTS
23	H B Myers	British	249cc Excelsior
24	E R Evans	British	249cc OK Supreme
25	R H Pike	British	249cc Rudge
26	S Woods	Irish	249cc Moto Guzzi
27	S M Miller	British	249cc CTS
29	E Kluge	German	248cc DKW
30	G V Dickwell	Belgian	246cc Benelli
31	J C Galway	S African	249cc Excelsior
32	J H White	British	249cc Excelsior

LIGHTWEIGHT FINISHERS

POS	NAME	MACHINE	TIME	AV SPEED
1	E A Mellors	Benelli	3.33.26.0	74.26
2	E Kluge	DKW	3:37.11.0	72.97
3	H G Tyrell-Smith	Excelsior	3:40.23.0	71.91
4	L G Martin	Excelsior	3:50.08.0	68.87
5	S Wünsche	DKW	3:50.25.0	68.78
6	C H Manders	Excelsior	3:56.48.0	66.93
7	H Hartley	Rudge	3:59.27.0	66.19
8	E R Thomas	DKW	4:00.48.0	65.81
9	S Wood	Rudge	4:03.41.0	65.04
10	C Tattersall	CTS	4:07.50.0	63.95
11	W H S Pike	Rudge	4:08.39.0	63.74
12	H C Lamacraft	Excelsior	4:11.58.0	62.9
13	J McCredie	Excelsior	4:15.33.0	62.02

SENIOR ENTRIES

NO	NAME	NATIONALITY	MACHINE
1	H L Daniell	British	499cc Norton
2	M D Whitworth	British	348cc Velocette
3	N Croft	British	490cc Norton
4	H Hartley	British	499cc Rudge
5	W T Tiffen	British	348cc Velocette
6	C F Brett	British	348cc Velocette
7	N Christmas	British	348cc Velocette
8	J Williams	British	490cc Norton
9	W F Rusk	British	498cc AJS
10	S Woods	Irish	499cc Velocette
11	K Bodmer	German	346cc NSU
12	T B Fortune	British	499cc Rudge
14	H G Tyrell-Smith	Irish	498cc Excelsior
15	C Redfearn	British	348cc Velocette
16	L V Perry	N Zealander	348cc Velocette
17	F L Frith	British	499cc Norton
18	S Wood	British	499cc Norton

SENIOR ENTRIES CONTINUED

SENIOR FINISHERS

NO	NAME	NATIONALITY	MACHINE
19	L J Archer	British	495cc Velocette
20	M Cann	British	496cc Moto Guzzi
21	J A Weddell	British	490cc Norton
22	E R Thomas	British	495cc Velocette
23	T Reid	British	494cc BMW
24	H B Myers	British	490cc Norton
25	E S Oliver	British	348cc Velocette
26	G H Hayden	British	348cc Velocette
27	F Vaasen	German	490cc Norton
28	E A Mellors	British	495cc Velocette
29	K Gall	German	494cc BMW
30	R J Weston	British	490cc Norton
31	N B Pope	British	490cc Norton
32	C H Manders	British	349cc Excelsior
33	J Lockett	British	499cc Norton
34	F W Fry	British	348cc Velocette
35	J M West	British	494cc BMW
36	F J Mussett	Australian	348cc Velocette
37	L A Dear	British	348cc Velocette
38	J E Little	British	348cc Velocette
39	H C Lamacraft	British	348cc Velocette
40	J C Galway	S African	499cc Norton
41	J K Boardman	British	490cc Norton
42	R Lampinen	Finnish	490cc Norton
43	F Anderson	British	346cc DKW
44	S M Miller	British	348cc Velocette
45	W H Craine	British	490cc Norton
46	W Herz	German	346cc NSU
47	J W Beevers	British	490cc Norton
48	A R Foster	British	498cc AJS
49	G Meier	German	494cc BMW
50	O Rührschneck	German	346cc NSU
51	J H White	British	499cc Norton
52	G Newman	British	348cc Velocette

POS	NAME	MACHINE	TIME	AV SPEED
1	G Meier	BMW	2.57.19.0	89.38
2	J M West	BMW	2:59.39.0	88.22
3	F L Frith	Norton	3:00.11.0	87.96
4	S Woods	Velocette	3:00.17.0	87.91
5	J H White	Norton	3:04.27.0	85.92
6	L J Archer	Velocette	3:07.58.0	84.31
7	E A Mellors	Velocette	3:09.12.0	83.76
8	S Wood	Norton	3:12.16.0	82.43
9	M Cann	Moto Guzzi	3:13.22.0	81.96
10	J C Galway	Norton	3:15.00.0	81.37
11	W F Rusk	AJS	3:16.30.0	80.65
12	M D Whitworth	Velocette	3:18.09.0	79.98
13	A R Foster	AJS	3:19.11.0	79.57
14	J E Little	Velocette	3:21.06.0	78.81
15	E R Thomas	Velocette	3:21.40.0	78.59
16	H C Lamacraft	Velocette	3:21.45.0	78.55
17	E S Oliver	Velocette	3:24.31.0	77.49
18	N B Pope	Norton	3:24.50.0	77.37
19	J W Beevers	Norton	3:25.07.0	77.26
20	N Croft	Norton	3:27.32.0	76.36
21	G Newman	Velocette	3:27.34.0	76.35
22	F W Fry	Velocette	3:27.51.0	76.25
23	W T Tiffen	Velocette	3:27.58.0	76.21
24	N Christmas	Velocette	3:28.23.0	76.05
25	J K Boardman	Norton	3:29.39.0	75.59
26	H B Myers	Norton	3:30.02.0	75.46
27	S M Miller	Velocette	3:32.09.0	74.7
28	F Anderson	DKW	3:32.57.0	74.42
29	H Hartley	Rudge	3:40.41.0	71.81
30	R J Weston	Norton	3:41.50.0	71.44

5 • DON'T MENTION IT

The countdown to conflict only had two and a half months to run at the end of the 1939 TT. And it seems incredible now that the European motorcycle racing season continued regardless during those last few weeks.

Fortified by Senior TT triumph, Schorsch Meier set about retaining his European 500cc championship title with gusto. Two weeks later he won the Dutch TT at Assen and followed that up with victory at Spa in Belgium – also claiming the first-ever 100mph lap of any Grand Prix circuit in the process. But missing the French Grand Prix to drive

for Auto Union in the car equivalent at Reims proved to be a mistake – although Crasher White won the French bike event for Norton rather than Meier's principal opponent, Italian star Dorino Serafini.

During the next round of the motorcycle championship at Saxtorp in Sweden, Meier crashed while chasing Serafini's supercharged four-cylinder Gilera and incurred a serious

◆ As war began, BMW put away its Kompressors for the duration and began developing products like the R75 (above) with entirely different performance parameters, self-evidently not always with the success the Nazis required.

spinal injury – bad enough to put him out for the rest of the season. Serafini went on to win the following two Grands Prix in Germany and Ulster as well. This was enough to steal the championship away because the Swiss and Italian rounds were cancelled.

Because both Meier and his BMW team-mate Wiggerl Kraus were side-lined out of the German home round of the European series by injury, the factory recruited Jock West as a stand-in. West reputedly accepted this ride – less than a month before military hostilities commenced – because he was still angling for a BMW Kompressor to defend his Ulster Grand Prix record. As it turned out he failed to finish the race, after his bike broke down while in close pursuit of Serafini. And BMW failed to supply a machine for the Ulster either. What the factory did do, however, was rush West and his wife back to Munich from the Sachsenring and get them on one of the last flights back to England – to avoid internment as enemy aliens.

Top DKW riders had better luck for their Zschopau factory. In the 350cc European championship, Heiner Fleischmann matched his third place in the Junior TT with similar results at Assen in Holland and then the Grand Prix of Europe at the Nürburgring back in Germany. But he won the French and Swedish rounds, and went into the final leg on the 20.5-mile Old Clady course in Ulster level on points with Velocette-mounted Ted Mellors.

As the last international motorcycle race held in Europe only a few days before the declaration of war, the Ulster Grand Prix that year attracted only 60 entries. But, as runner-up behind Stanley Woods in the 350 race, Fleischmann took the championship for Germany despite a 93.54mph fastest lap from Mellors. Fleischmann had also found time to add a third German national 350 title to his roll of honour during the season.

Considering the date of that final European event, the DKW team must have got out of Ulster by the skin of their teeth – probably by deftly swerving over the nearby border to catch a boat home from neutral Eire rather than returning via Belfast and through the UK.

Ewald Kluge more firmly dominated the European 250 series for the second year in succession and took his fourth consecutive German national title in the class. Sissi Wünsche, meanwhile, finished third on that final Ulster podium and also third in the European 350 championship – behind Mellors – for his second year in a row.

But for NSU the news was not good. Given the rapidly deteriorating political climate, its British chief design engineer Walter Moore resigned from the company and declined to return to Neckarsulm after the TT. Wilhelm Herz, Karl Bodmer and Otto Rührschneck soldiered on in European and German national racing aboard Moore and Röder's blown twin to no apparent benefit. The machine was too heavy, poor handling and terminally unreliable. Röder had already fallen out with Moore over its shortcomings and left NSU to join Victoria as chief engineer. Herz later said that he thought the supercharged project had development potential but the bike needed substantial changes.

Hitler had briefed his military high command about requirements for the next portion of Lebensraum strategic application in May 1939. As a result, the Nazis had begun amassing several vast Army groups facing the Polish border during the summer and started high-altitude military reconnaissance flights over Poland in early August. And that country's future – or lack of it – became subject of two pivotal diplomatic agreements.

At the end of March 1939, Britain and France had guaranteed Polish sovereignty, and then on 25 August a Polish-British Common Defence Pact was signed. But Germany had already put ink to paper on the Molotov-Ribbentrop Pact – a non-aggression deal with the USSR – on 23 August. A secret protocol within this agreement allowed for the mutual carving up of Poland. The Russians therefore wouldn't intervene on the other side (the very opposite, in fact) and the Nazis knew that Britain and France were strategically, tactically and logistically incapable of coming to Poland's defence in any meaningful way.

Hitler had been pursuing another diplomatic ploy against Poland for some time. This involved demanding the return of the Baltic port of Danzig – which had a predominantly German population but was a 'free' city under League of Nations control – and the right to build a German road through the Polish territorial corridor separating Germany from its East Prussian enclave. British Prime Minister Neville Chamberlain and remaining appeasement lackeys had been pressing Poland to give in on these proposals for months – and reportedly still regarded the German terms as 'reasonable' on 29 August 1939.

The time for diplomatic smokescreens was over, though. On 31 August, Hitler ordered his combined forces to attack Poland in the early hours of the following morning. On 1 September at 4.45am, around 2000 tanks organised into five Panzer divisions rolled over the border to spearhead the Wehrmacht ground invasion. The Luftwaffe filled the skies with indiscriminate terror-bombing raids on Polish cities and the Kriegsmarine battle cruiser Schleswig-Holstein began shelling Polish troop emplacements on the Westerplatte peninsula near Danzig. Two days later, on 3 September, Britain and France honoured their treaty obligations by declaring war on Germany. Then, on 17 September, the Russians invaded Poland from the east to claim their share of the spoils. By 1 October the country had ceased to exist. The Second World War had begun in earnest and motorcycle racing - apart, oddly, from the Italian national championship – ground to a halt for the duration.

As in Britain, the German motorcycle industry was turned over wholly to manufacturing military-oriented products. At NSU, Baron Fritz von Falkenhayn remained as managing director throughout the war until 1945. However, production at the Neckarsulm factory necessarily ceased in 1944 after the Royal Air Force comprehensively bombed it out of business.

As his most memorable contribution to the Nazi war effort, Falkenhayn played an instrumental role in the creation of the unique NSU Kleines Kettenkrad HK101. Its name derived from Ketten (referring to track-laying) and an abbreviation of Kraftrad (referring to motorcycles), and it was basically half of each. The body of the Kettenkrad had

◆ NSU's showpiece product during the Second World War was the versatile Kleines Kettenkrad HK101 all-terrain battlefield tractor (above). Powered by an Opel car engine, this had been originally designed to tow artillery or ammunition trailers but was later used for a plethora of military purposes.

twin caterpillar tracks like a miniature tank, powered by a four-cylinder 1500cc Opel car engine. But a motorcycle headstock, handlebar, forks and front wheel had been grafted on to provide steering. This operated just like a bike if small handlebar movements were used to change direction. When the going got tough and riders had to make sharper steering movements, linkages to the fork applied the appropriate track brake at the rear to facilitate turning.

The Kettenkrad was conceived as a battlefield tractor to pull light artillery or ammunition trailers over difficult terrain. Because its original specification was for airborne troops, compact scale was necessary so it would fit in the cargo bay of a Junkers Ju 52 transport aeroplane – although it wasn't designed to be dropped by parachute. Obvious versatility meant that it acquired many other roles. In the cloying mud of the Eastern Front it was even pressed into service as a pocket-sized troop carrier and the Luftwaffe employed Kettenkrads as runway tractors for towing aircraft.

◆ If a particular selling point of BMW's 255 Kompressor race bike in the late 1930s was its ability to gallop along at more than 130mph, then the R75 military combination launched in 1942 (top and above) was an entirely different kettle of sauerkraut. One of its key design features was that it could be ridden at goose-stepping pace – about 2mph – alongside troops on the march without overheating. Other features were two-wheel drive for off-road use and the capacity to carry three stormtroopers with all their weapons, ammunition and equipment. Its tyres were also interchangeable with those fitted to the Wehrmacht's ubiquitous Kublewagen light utility vehicle – which was based on the rear-engined Volkswagen 'people's car'.

During the war, BMW squirrelled away its stable of 255 Kompressor race bikes at Berg on Lake Starnberg, south of Munich. Schorsch Meier reportedly managed to expropriate his TT-winning machine from this collection in 1943 and subsequently hid it in a barn in the Allacher forest, near Karlsfeld – not far from either the Dachau concentration camp or the BMW factory at Allach in the outskirts of Munich. And in sharp contrast to the Kompressor's advanced technology, BMW's initial input to Wehrmacht war requirements was its long-in-the-tooth R12, with a 750cc side-valve boxer motor and rigid pressed-steel frame. This antiquity stayed in production until 1942, when it was replaced by a much cleverer, purpose-designed military motorcycle called the R75.

Essentially meant to be the motive component in a sidecar outfit, the OHV R75 could be ridden at marching pace – about 2mph – without overheating, featured low-ratio gearing for off-road use, an additional drive shaft with differential to the sidecar wheel and reverse gear. It was capable of carrying three soldiers and all their equipment. BMW built about 18,000 of these bikes, most of which were subsequently destroyed in action. Some 6000 were assembled at Munich before motorcycle production was moved to Eisenach, west of Leipzig, to make way for aero engine manufacturing. But, as with NSU at Neckarsulm, BMW's Eisenach factory was eventually brought to a standstill in 1944 by American aerial bombing which flattened 60 per cent of it.

DKW also focused on utilitarian two-stroke military machinery for Wehrmacht consumption such as the NZ350-1 and NZ250-1. Like BMW's wartime products, these were a far cry from the company's hi-tech race equipment. The 350cc version produced a hardly rip-snorting maximum power output of 11.5bhp at 4000rpm. Large numbers of the now-legendary RT125 were also churned out in Wehrmacht livery. This bike rates as the most-copied in history because sets of blueprints were confiscated in the guise of war reparations by the Americans, Russians and British in 1945. The resultant US knock-off was the Harley-Davidson

Hummer, BSA christened its version the Bantam and the Soviet take was called a Voshkod. At least the DKW motorcycle factory in Zschopau escaped Allied air raids – unlike nearby Dresden, which was controversially and fairly gratuitously bombed to the point of obliteration by the RAF – and also remained intact before and after the Soviet army finally gang-raped its way through Saxony.

With the end of motorcycle and motor sport, the NSKK lost any Nazi propaganda function but continued its training and motorised transport roles in support of the Wehrmacht and SS in German-occupied countries. An element of this was providing vehicles and drivers to facilitate Hitler's 'Final Solution of the Jewish Question'. The NSKK was also involved in Aktion T4, another extermination programme designed to eliminate psychiatric and incurably-ill hospital patients, as well as congenitally disabled people. More than 70,000 German men, women and children were murdered during Aktion T4, for which the NSKK reportedly provided secure buses to move victims to extermination centres and developed sealed ambulances where the exhaust system could be diverted through the interior to kill them by carbon monoxide poisoning – so it was unquestionably participating in genocidal war crimes.

NSKK-Korpsführer Adolf Hühnlein died of natural causes at the age of 61 on 18 June 1942. He was honoured with a state funeral and posthumously awarded the highest Third Reich accolade, the Deutschen Orden. Almost exactly three years after his return from commanding operations at the Isle of Man TT in 1939, Obergruppenführer Erwin Kraus was elevated to Korpsführer as Hühnlein's successor.

The five German racers returning home from the 1939 TT who weren't already fully militarised – Ewald Kluge, Heinrich Fleischmann, Karl Bodmer, Otto Rührschneck and Wilhelm Herz – moved into the Wehrmacht from the NSKK as war began. Georg Meier and Seigfried Wünsche, both already Reichswehr regulars, simply returned to their units. But it's interesting to note that their Nazi propaganda star status generally earned them cushy jobs well away from combat zones for most of the war.

◆ The Wehrmacht probably regarded very basic military motorcycles like the two-stroke DKW NZ 350 (top and above) as preferable to BMW offerings – not least because they were much cheaper to manufacture. And their simplicity also meant they were far easier to maintain and repair in less-than-perfect wartime conditions. As a result, they were some of the most common workhorses employed by the Nazis in all theatres of operations.

◆ Newly promoted NSKK-Korpsführer Erwin Kraus (above, second from right) discussing the involvement of his organisation in the construction of defences on the Western Front – the French coastline, in other words – in August 1942 with Reichswehr officers. The NSKK's motorcycle sports propaganda role had become surplus to Nazi requirements by then and he was busy with its remaining task of motorising the war effort.

DKW star and confirmed Nazi Ewald Kluge exchanged his altogether grander-sounding NSKK-Stürmführer paramilitary rank for that of an Unteroffizier (corporal) in charge of a unit training motorcycle despatch riders. He was initially based in Leipzig and then at the Schule für Heeresmotorisierung (school for military motorisation) attached to Wehrmacht High Command headquarters in Wünsdorf, 40km south of Berlin. But at the request of DKW parent Auto Union he was given leave of absence from Wehrmacht duties in 1943 to become a test rider for the R&D department back at DKW's Zschopau factory.

In an area that was squeezed between advancing US and Soviet forces in 1945, Kluge foolishly failed to join Wehrmacht stragglers beating a hasty retreat westwards away from the River Elbe to surrender to the Americans. He was instead captured by the Russians. In 1946 he was denounced in front of a 'denazification' tribunal for his pre-war NSKK and Nazi Party activism, for which he received an invigorating three-year sentence in a Soviet labour camp.

The war service of Kluge's team-mates Heinrich Fleischmann and Siegfried Wünsche was less remarkable. Both survived unscathed but Fleischmann took longer to reappear afterwards, because he probably had some 'denazification' problems of his own. Chickens came home to roost and having been photographed strutting about with Kluge in full NSKK paramilitary uniform at high-profile Nazi propaganda presentations in 1939 – something he later tried to deny having done despite the evidence – was hard to live down.

After joining the Wehrmacht, NSU rider Karl Bodmer was also posted to the military motorisation school in Wünsdorf as a motorcycle instructor in 1940. But he obviously didn't have Kluge's Nazi connections to stay in a plum posting, because in 1943 he was reassigned to the nearby Panzertruppenschule to be trained as a tank commander. Promoted to Feldwebel, Bodmer was then sent to the Eastern Front where he fought against the Russians in some of the most cataclysmic combat conditions imaginable for two years. He was badly wounded by phosphorus grenade

◆ Respectively 1939 Junior and Lightweight TT podium placemen Heiner Fleischmann (above far left) and Ewald Kluge (above far right) being interviewed during a Nazi propaganda event in Berlin – trashing Fleischmann's later denial that he was ever a paramilitary activist. The black-uniformed SS officer is Auto Union car racing driver Hans Stuck.

splinters in his left arm just before the end of the war and shipped home on a stretcher. His NSU team-mate Wilhelm Herz also survived Wehrmacht service and capture, and was eventually released from an American prisoner-of-war camp in 1946.

Senior TT victor Georg Meier probably had the best war out of the lot. Following several months of convalescence due to the injuries he'd collected when crashing out of the 1939 Swedish Grand Prix, he returned to light non-combatant duties as a military police motorcycle instructor. Shortly afterwards he was appointed as personal driver to Abwehr military intelligence chief Admiral Wilhelm Canaris and acquired status as Oberfeldwebel (sergeant-major) in charge of the Abwehr's transport section.

To assume that Canaris was an avowed Nazi would be wildly wrong. Although a Nazi appointee as Abwehr supremo from 1935 onwards, he had become disillusioned with Hitler three years later and began covertly conspiring against the Third Reich. He first made contact with the British secret intelligence service MI6 in 1939 through his like-minded associate Ewald von Kleist-Schmenzin – who

◆ Abwehr military intelligence head Admiral Wilhelm Canaris (top) – for whom 1939 Senior TT winner Schorsh Meier became personal driver for most of the war – was actually the most senior British MI6 agent within the Nazi hierachy. Meier, who was also promoted to Oberfeldwebel in charge of the Abwehr's transport section, later claimed to have never taken the Nazis seriously – but seemed extraordinarily smug about being presented to the Führer (above).

visited London on behalf of both of them – and from that point on was, to all intents and purposes, a British agent. His false rumour about an impending Nazi invasion of Holland in early 1939 – mentioned in Chapter One – was probably a put-up job by MI6, eager to blow the wind of war up its own government's skirt by any means necessary.

Canaris was involved in a wide range of spying and black propaganda activities for the British, as well as various well-documented plots against Hitler and the Nazi regime. Amazingly, he remained entirely above suspicion until 1942. Reichsführer-SS Heinrich Himmler and SS-Obergruppenführer Reinhard Heydrich – chief of the SS counter-intelligence service known as the SD and the Gestapo – had begun to smell a rat by then. The MI6-orchestrated assassination of Heydrich in Prague on 27 May 1942 was partially motivated by the need to protect Canaris from too-rigorous investigation.

Nevertheless he was being watched closely by the SD. Suspicions of his betrayal grew and Himmler finally managed to persuade Hitler to sack him and merge the SD and Abwehr under a new SS-appointed chief in February 1944. Canaris was placed under house arrest a few weeks later and subsequently imprisoned by the Gestapo after circumstantial evidence linked him to the 20 July plot to assassinate Hitler that year. Ironically, NSU managing director and enthusiastic Nazi Baron Fritz von Falkenhayn's younger sister Erika was married to another of the plotters, General Henning von Tresckow, who committed suicide after their bomb failed to kill the Führer.

Meier made a big noise after the war about never having been a member of the Nazi Party. But as a Reichswehr regular soldier he was actually forbidden to join it by military regulations. Similarly he stressed that he'd never belonged to the NSKK – although he didn't have to because his police and army career predated the NSKK's foundation, and Wehrmacht personnel tended to sneer at paramilitaries as inferior anyway. However, to get the posting as driver for such a senior figure in the first place and keep it once the Abwehr was being infiltrated by SD men monitoring

Canaris meant he must have been trusted. And the only people Nazis felt comfortable with were those demonstrably loyal to their cause. Meier had also been presented to the Führer in person after winning the Senior TT in 1939 – wearing his Reichswehr uniform, of course – not a privilege accorded to many comparatively junior Feldwebels.

One German motorcycle racer was less lucky. Although he had escaped over the border into Holland in 1938, with the promise of emigrating to an engineering job in a Brazilian motorcycle assembly plant, the racially unhygienic former DKW works rider Leo Steinweg got no further than that. His sub-standard 'Jewish' passport had been confiscated by the Dutch police so he and his wife Emmy – who had joined him in 1939 – were unable to leave. They were still trapped there when the Blitzkrieg was inflicted on the Low Countries in May 1940.

Leo and Emmy Steinweg were hidden from the Nazis on the top floor of a house in Utrecht's Hartingstraat by Dutch resistance fighters for two years after the Nazi occupation. They were eventually arrested in a Gestapo raid on 28 August 1942. After a period of imprisonment in Holland at the Durchgangslager Westerbork – a transit camp where the famous Jewish child diarist Ann Frank was also temporarily incarcerated in 1944 – Leo Steinweg was put on a train to Konzentrationslager Auschwitz-Birkenau, 50 miles west of Kraków in Poland. His wife stayed on in Holland.

Largest of all Nazi concentration and extermination camp complexes, Auschwitz was in full murderously industrial swing when Steinweg arrived. By the end of the war, more than a million inmates had been executed in its gas chambers – most of them Jews. But he presumably avoided the lungful of Zyklon-B and one-way ticket to the crematorium that was mandatory for most new arrivals by then because he had useful skills. The fact that he was a 'name' prisoner may have also helped. Whatever, Steinweg spent the next two years servicing and repairing motorcycles and cars for the SS guards there.

Reichsführer-SS Heinrich Himmler ordered the evacuation and destruction of KZ Auschwitz in November

◆ NSU managing director Baron Fritz von Falkenhayn's brother-in-law Reichswehr General Henning von Tresckow (top) was a co-conspirator with Canaris in the failed 20 July plot to kill Hitler. He chose to commit suicide rather than face arrest. The view back towards the gatehouse of KZ Auschwitz-Birkenau (above) that former DKW works motorcycle racer Leo Steinweg would have seen after arrival on a deportation train from Holland.

◆ Early Nazi genocide methods (above), involved excessive ammunition consumption and poor productivity necessitated by the digging of mass graves – work usually carried out by the victims. So the 'Final Solution' was fast-tracked with industrialisation via purpose-built gas chambers and crematoria at vast extermination camps like KZ Auschwitz-Birkenau. Some NSKK stormtroopers were explicitly involved in building and servicing them.

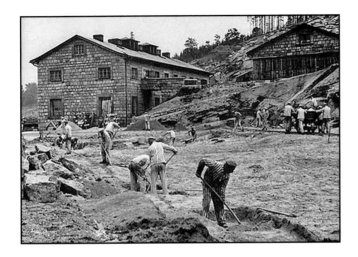

◆ Slave labourers at KZ Flossenbürg (left), where Jewish motorcycle racer Leo Steinweg and Abwehr head Admiral Canaris were among 1500 special prisoners murdered in 1945 on Himmler's orders, just weeks before the end of the war. Allied troops liberating the concentration camps were met by horrific scenes of degradation, starvation and death (above left). Nazi cynicism about the Holocaust was extraordinary – the Arbeit Macht Frei sign above the main gate into KZ Auschwitz (above right) translates as 'work makes you free'.

1944, to conceal the evidence of what had gone on there from advancing Soviet forces. In early January 1945 about 60,000 of the remaining prisoners were sent on a forced death march towards another camp in Poland – KZ Loslau. A further 20,000 were transferred by train to KZ Bergen-Belsen. And a number of potentially useful 'name' prisoners, including Steinweg and various captured enemy intelligence agents, were moved to KZ Flossenbürg, just inside Germany close to the old Czech border. When KZ Auschwitz-Birkenau was finally liberated by the 322nd Rifle Division of the Soviet Army on 27 January 1945 there were only about 7500 surviving inmates left.

Himmler had gathered together such 'names' at KZ Flossenbürg to use as bargaining counters in a negotiated ceasefire or conditional surrender that might get him off the hook. Apart from Steinweg, former Abwehr head Wilhelm Canaris – previously Georg Meier's eminent passenger – was sent there too.

But by the end of March Himmler realised there was going to be no deal with the Allies and instructed KZ Flossenbürg commandant SS-Stürmbahnführer Max Koegel to tidy the place up. Some 22,000 people including 1700 Jews, mainly slave labourers from the Flossenbürg camp quarries, were force-marched south to KZ Dachau near Munich. More than 7000 of them were shot dead by SS guards for failing to keep up along the way, or collapsed and died from starvation before reaching their destination.

Then on 23 April – only three days after the majority of the prisoners and their Nazi tormentors had marched out – the US 90th Infantry Division arrived. They found about 1600 survivors, ill and starving, in the hospital barracks – evidently deemed not worth a waste of valuable ammunition.

Leo Steinweg and Wilhelm Canaris weren't among them, or among the living or dead en route to Dachau. Along with all the other now-inconvenient 'names' they had been murdered on Himmler's orders and their bodies cremated about two weeks earlier, before the SS abandoned Flossenbürg. Steinweg's nemesis, camp commandant Koegel, was sentenced to death at the Nuremberg War Crimes Tribunal in 1946 but cheated the hangman's noose by committing suicide. Himmler escaped trial because he had also committed suicide some months earlier, following his arrest by the Allies at Lüneberg.

6 • WE'LL MEET AGAIN

Quite rightly given he was on the winning side, BMW's runner-up in the 1939 TT Jock West prospered mightily during and after the war. Commissioned as an officer in the Royal Air Force, he applied his engineering experience to developing fast-turnaround repair facilities for aircraft damaged in combat. At the end of hostilities in 1945, West had risen to the rank of Wing Commander and was awarded the OBE for his efforts.

Returning to civilian life, he became sales manager of Matchless and AJS manufacturer Associated Motor Cycles (AMC) based at Plumstead in South London, and briefly resumed his bike racing career as well. AMC had spent the war churning out more than 80,000 utilitarian Matchless G3 machines for the army and in that post-war period of austerity with most resources rationed was hardly in a position to invest in new race bikes. So his first notably successful outing in 1946 was victory on a distinctly pre-war AJS 500cc water-cooled V4 at Chimay in Belgium. However, AMC also revived another pre-war project that had never come to fruition. This was the AJS E90S 'Porcupine', and West gave it a baptism of fire in the 1947 Senior TT – at the first TT meeting held since 1939.

The E90S was highly advanced, a double-overhead-camshaft 500cc horizontal parallel twin that had been supercharged in its prototype form. But forced induction was banned by the FIM international motorcycle sports authority from 1946 onwards. The Porcupine nickname came from prominent finning on its forward-facing cylinder head. Also novel for the time were unit-construction crankcases with an integral gearbox. Suspension was state-of-the-art too, with hydraulically-damped telescopic forks at the front and similarly damped twin shocks and swingarm at the rear.

The bike was barely ready in time to go to the Island and its only test run had been a quick blast down the A2 main road into Kent near AMC's factory a couple of weeks earlier. Inevitably it was afflicted with teething problems. Although West managed to claim the third-fastest lap of the race at 84mph, he eventually crossed the line in 14th place – last of the finishers – more than an hour behind winner Harold Daniell's Norton with an overall race average of barely 61mph. His luck didn't improve at the Ulster Grand Prix later that year either, as more technical problems pushed him a long way off the leaderboard.

Returning to the Isle of Man in 1948 for the last time as a race contender, West debuted the new AJS 7R 350cc OHC single – taking 13th place in the Junior – and then broke down in the Senior on the Porcupine. But he'd had enough and, as his 40th birthday approached, took the decision to retire from racing at the end of that season. His swansong appearance on the Porcupine was at the banked Montlhery track in France, where he, Les Graham and Frenchman Georges Monneret took six 500cc world speed endurance records. Graham went on to win the 1949 500cc world championship on a Porcupine.

Jock West rose to become group sales director of AMC as it acquired further marques – James and Francis-Barnett, and finally Norton. But he got tired of fighting narrow-minded fellow managers as the British motorcycle industry plunged into decline and resigned in 1961. AMC went bust

◆ Eight years after the war, Siegfried 'Sissi' Wünsche returned to the Isle of Man and scored his best-ever TT result in the 1953 Lightweight on the 250cc twin-cylinder version of a completely new generation of DKW two-stroke race bikes (facing page, left). He was the only 1930s-vintage former NSKK paramilitary stormtrooper to reappear on Manx shores as a competitor.

◆ 1939 Senior TT victor Georg 'Schorsh' Meier (above) – seen here with his Kompressor in old age – enjoyed a very successful bike racing career after the war, with a total of five German national championship titles. He then went on to prosper as a BMW car and motorcycle dealer in Starnberg south of Munich, a business that still bears his name and is run by his descendants.

in 1966. After leaving AMC, West joined the board of a leading motorcycle accessories wholesaler of the day – Glanfield Lawrence – before moving on to become sales director of the UK Lambretta scooter distributor. He finally finished his career back with BMW, working for the British concessionaire. He enjoyed a long retirement and died aged 95 on 9 June 2004 – during TT race week that year.

After a short period of internment as 'surrendered enemy personnel', West's team-mate Schorsch Meier went home to Munich and initially got a job as a security guard at BMW's Allach factory, which was being used as a transport centre by the US Army. But it didn't take him long to get back on a race bike. Germany was excluded from participating in international motor and motorcycle sports competition after the war until 1951 but 'denazified' racing at a national level was revived by 1947. Meier had retrieved

his 255 Kompressor from its hiding place and was on the tracks that year. His first post-war appearance at the 11.4km Solitudering roads circuit near Stuttgart attracted more than a quarter of a million spectators.

Exclusion by the FIM meant German racers didn't have to comply with the forced-induction ban on home turf and continuing development of the Kompressor made it – and Meier – utterly dominant in the German championship. During that period, the bike acquired various supercharger improvements, aluminium cylinder barrels, and a lighter crank and conrods – allegedly taking power up to 95bhp in its final incarnation. Meier acquired four consecutive German 500cc series titles from 1947 to 1950 as a result, and was hailed as German Sportsman of the Year in 1949.

His exploits were a big promotional benefit to BMW, which had got back into motorcycle mass production at the end of 1948. However, Allied occupation restrictions limited the factory to making machines with a maximum capacity of 250cc. So the relaunch product was a modest 12bhp single-cylinder bike called the R23 rather than BMW's trademark boxer-twin configuration.

Meier clearly didn't get on too well with the normally-aspirated boxer-twin race bike that replaced the Kompressor in 1951, because his much younger BMW factory team-mate Walter Zeller took the national title off him that year. And Rudi Knees won it on a Norton in 1952. But, appropriately, in his final year of racing Meier snatched the 500cc German national championship back for BMW in 1953.

Retirement from racing allowed Meier to cash in on his fame by building up a successful BMW motorcycle and car dealership. It's still there and still run by his family, in Starnberg south of Munich, but now only sells the BMW and MINI car brands. Understandably, he maintained good relations with the BMW factory throughout the rest of his life, featuring prominently in an advertising campaign to celebrate the marque's 60th year of bike production in 1983 and then returning for a parade lap around the Island on his Kompressor in 1989 to commemorate the 50th anniversary of Nazi TT victory. He died in February 1999 at the age of 89.

The post-war return of leading DKW-mounted riders was hindered by a number of problems – not least of which was that the marque's Zschopau factory was in the Soviet occupation zone and in the process of expropriation by East German communists. It was to be transformed into the home of IFA and then MZ motorcycles. However, DKW parent Auto Union re-registered itself in West Germany and opened a new factory at Ingolstadt on the Danube in Upper Bavaria. This began to produce RT125 road bikes in 1949 and was running works race machinery again the following year.

The other obvious difficulty was that one of the marque's loyalist star riders, former NSKK-Obertruppführer Ewald Kluge, was paying the price of his unsavoury Nazi past in jail until 1949. And Heiner Fleischmann, DKW's 1939 350cc European champion, had jumped ship back to NSU. So it was initially left to Sissi Wünsche and pre-war DKW 500cc campaigner and 1936 national champion Hermann Paul 'Happi' Müller to raise the two-stroke banner again as privateers. Müller's DKW took the German 250 national title in 1947 and 1948. Wünsche managed to buy a SS 350 supercharged split-twin in 1948 and ended up third in his championship class. The following year he won it and was second in 1950 – by which time he'd been recruited by the resurgent factory again.

With a works contract, Wünsche was up the sharp end of German national racing in the 250 and 350 classes in 1951 and 1952. In the second of those years, DKW unveiled all-new 250 twin and 350 triple machinery designed by Erich Wolf, and returned to the international stage – now a world rather than European championship. Then in 1953 Wünsche became the only pre-war NSKK stormtrooper to make another attempt at the Isle of Man TT.

He came equipped with these new bikes – a 250 parallel twin for the Lightweight and a 350 V3 with two vertical outer cylinders and a horizontal centre cylinder for the Junior. Although very fast, the early versions of this triple were notoriously fragile because they were under-engineered to reduce weight. It was eventually redesigned to be more durable (and powerful) by Wolf's replacement Hellmut

◆ Sissi Wünsche's return as a DKW factory rider at the 1953 TT was rather less satisfactory in the Junior (top), where he failed to finish aboard the notoriously fragile 350cc triple designed by Erich Wolf. His last visit to the Isle of Man was in 1988 (above), for a gloriously noisy parade lap on his pre-war supercharged split single as the only survivor of the 1938 DKW squad, celebrating the 50th anniversary of his late team-mate Ewald Kluge's sensational Lightweight victory.

◆ More than half a century on from his first attempt at the TT, Sissi Wünsche (above, centre, with microphone) was feted like all such veterans during his final 1988 visit to the Island – all Nazi connections apparently long-forgotten. On the extreme right – a position that doesn't necessarily reflect his ideological stance – is leading Manx politician Adrian Earnshaw, formerly the Isle of Man's Minister for Tourism and Leisure and more recently Minister for Home Affairs, trying to pick up a few tips on how to establish the Thousand-Year Tynwald.

Georg and was a serious world championship challenger in 1955 and 1956. But in 1953 it certainly wasn't up to tackling the TT and inevitably broke down. Wünsche had better luck on it in the German 350 championship that year, taking his second national title.

The Lightweight TT was a different story. Ater sitting a close fourth behind Guzzi-mounted Enrico Lorenzetti for two laps, Wünsche moved up to third when the Italian broke down and held station to the flag – achieving his best-ever Manx result and sole podium with an impressive race average of 81.34mph. The winner was his Scottish former DKW team-mate in 1939, Fergus Anderson, for Moto Guzzi with Werner Haas second for NSU.

Siegfried Wünsche retired from racing at the end of the 1955 season but later returned to the Isle of Man to ride TT parade laps in 1985 and 1988 – the last of these on a 1930s-vintage DKW. He died in August 2000 aged 84.

Having served his sentence and been shriven of Nazi connections, Ewald Kluge rejoined Wünsche at the DKW factory in 1950. But he was 41 years old by then and past his best. Nevertheless he delivered some notable results on the marque's new machinery in 1952.

At the spring meeting in Hanover's Eilenriede forest, he took victory with a record-breaking race average of 78.6mph on the 350 triple in front of more than 130,000 spectators. And in the German Grand Prix at the Solitudering, he came fourth in the 250 class and fifth on the 350. Kluge was credited with, respectively, 13th and 11th for the capacity classes in overall world championship standings at the end of that season thanks to these results.

But that 1952 250 GP had been won for DKW by Rudi Felgenheier who, along with his team-mate August Hobl, represented a much younger generation of German motorcycle racers. Kluge was having to try harder to get anywhere. Nevertheless he planned a return to the Isle of Man TT in 1953 as Wünsche's team-mate and appeared in that year's TT programme as entered on number 39 in the Junior – but he never made it to the Island again.

Two weeks before the TT, Kluge crashed very heavily while holding second place in the Eifel race at the Nürburgring. A resultant badly broken left leg ended his career. Ewald Kluge died of cancer in August 1964, aged 55. The commemorative street named after him, Ewald-Kluge-Strasse, is in Weixdorf on the outskirts of Dresden.

The young Rudi Felgenheier was drafted in by DKW to take over Kluge's 1953 TT ride and race number. He and Wünsche arrived late in practice week and, without any Mountain Course experience, Felgenheier was pathetically slow in his first session. So on the evening of 5 June before Saturday's final practice he went out to ride as many familiarisation laps as he could on a road bike. Just before the 30th Milestone, approaching the Verandah, he collided with a lorry coming the other way. A broken shoulder and severe leg and arm injuries suffered in that accident finished his race career too – and left Sissi Wünsche as DKW's sole campaigner on the Island.

DKW pulled out of motorcycle racing at the end of the 1956 season. Its parent Auto Union was acquired by Mercedes manufacturer Daimler Benz in 1957 and bike production stopped the following year. Volkswagen then bought Auto Union in 1964. Two-stroke DKW cars remained in production until 1966 and a light van until 1968, after which the marque was phased out. The factory site at Ingolstadt is now the headquarters of Audi, another of the original Auto Union companies.

Unlike BMW and DKW, the NSU factory in Neckarsulm swiftly patched up its bomb damage and was back in business almost immediately after the war. Recovery was helped to a great extent by a vehicle repair contract from the US Army occupation forces. Albert Röder returned as chief design engineer in 1947. Developments of the pre-war supercharged DOHC twin were soon on the stocks in 350cc and 500cc configurations, with the latter claiming 98bhp. Known as the Rennmax, it quickly became a winner.

As for the three members of NSU's factory team at the Nazi TT, Otto Rührschneck never resurfaced in motorcycle racing after the war, and may have been one of more than five million German combatants who perished during

hostilities. His brother Karl – who had ridden for BMW in the 1939 German championship – showed up again, though, as passenger in Sepp Müller's winning BMW sidecar outfit in the 1948 and 1949 national series.

Karl Bodmer did return to race for NSU again, helping to organise and entering some of the earliest events held in Germany during 1946. He then performed well on a blown 350 in the revived 1947 German national championship. But increasingly troubled by his wounded arm – which doctors had at one point considered amputating – he appeared less often in 1948 and then only in minor events. Retiring from racing that year, Bodmer went on to establish a large motorcycle and car dealership but his health declined steadily and he died in November 1955 aged only 44.

Undoubtedly the most successful – and well-known – of the NSU TT veterans was Wilhelm Herz. Racing again in 1947, Herz won the 350 German championship in 1948 on his supercharged NSU twin and went on to play a leading role in making NSU into a major racing name again. Riding a later range of normally-aspirated Sportmax machinery, his young protégé Werner Haas won both the 125cc and 250cc world championships in 1953 and then the 250 title again in 1954. The 44-year-old DKW veteran Happi Müller even came over to NSU to win the 1955 250 world title and join Herz in his other famous sporting enterprise – world motorcycle speed records – in 1956.

Wilhelm Herz originally took the outright motorcycle speed record in 1951 on a 500cc version of the supercharged Rennmax. Averaged out of two runs over a closed section of the Bundesautobahn 45 motorway between Munich and Ingolstadt, he managed to hit 180.29mph. But that wasn't fast enough for Herz, because in 1956 he and Müller set off for Bonneville Salt Flats in Utah armed with fully-enclosed streamliners powered by NSU engines. On his 500 Rennmax, Herz this time reached 211.4mph – the first man to exceed 200mph in any record attempt on two wheels. He was as fast as modern MotoGP bikes more than 50 years ago.

Müller, meanwhile, took three more world records on a lightweight 'flying deckchair' streamliner designed by

Gustav Baumm. This was powered by a selection of tuned small-capacity engines from NSU's road range. The 50cc version achieved an amazing 121.7mph; a 100cc motor got to 137.9mph; and a 125 reached 150.3mph.

Two years before, in 1954, Herz had become managing director of the Hockenheim race circuit – beginning a reign that lasted 38 years. He was subsequently responsible for developing the track into one of the greatest motorcycle and car racing venues in Europe and was widely feted for his efforts at the highest level. He eventually retired at the ripe old age of 80 in 1992 and died just six years later in January 1998. A street name in Hockenheim, Wilhelm-Herz-Strasse, preserves his memory.

DKW's 1939 Junior TT star Heiner Fleischmann, who had won three German 350 championships before the war – two of them for NSU – also returned to the marque. Riding its 350cc and 500cc supercharged bikes in the domestic

◆ Although the 1953 TT programme listed pre-war Nazi Ewald Kluge as riding on the number 39 plate in that year's Junior, he was lying injured in a German hospital and it was actually DKW's last-minute replacement Rudi Felgenheier out in practice (facing page, left). While his 1939 TT performance had been less than spectacular, NSU factory rider Wilhelm Herz and the Rennmax streamliner (top) created a major landmark in motorcycling history in 1956 by breaking the 200mph world speed record barrier on two wheels at Bonneville Salt Flats.

series again from 1948 onwards, his best year was 1950 – the swansong for blowers before Germany was allowed back into international motorcycle sport and therefore had to comply with FIM regulations.

During that early post-war period, the national championship was pan-German for four years, with rounds in both East and West Germany. Fleischmann went to the final 1950 event at the Sachsenring in what had become the German Democratic Republic communist dictatorship in 1949 and ruled the roost. In the 350 race he beat DKW's Sissi Wünsche to take his fourth championship title in that class. And then on the 500cc Rennmax, he thrashed a somewhat-surprised Schorsch Meier too. Fleischmann took the race but Meier still had the 500 title for BMW.

NSU started to concentrate on smaller-capacity Sportmax machinery in 1951, so there was no works deal for Fleischmann in Neckarsulm after that year and he ended his competition career shortly afterwards. He died from throat cancer five weeks before his 50th birthday on Christmas Day 1963. But Neckarsulm didn't forget him and you can eat a McDonalds burger or buy an Iveco truck on that city's Heiner-Fleischmann-Strasse.

Another member of the Nazi TT cohort also reappeared at NSU in 1953, when Baron Fritz von Falkenhayn was judged to be sufficiently 'denazified' and invited to become a director of the company again. Falkenhayn remained on the NSU supervisory board until 1961. The company ceased motorcycle production in 1963 and then paupered itself building classy but mechanically inept Wankel-engined RO80 cars until swallowed by Volkswagen in 1969. Baron von Falkenhayn died in March 1973.

At the time of writing this book in early 2009, the solitary surviving character of any significance in it – with impressive irony – is erstwhile Jewish motorcycle racer Leo Steinweg's wife Emmy.

She remained in Holland for the rest of the war following his arrest in 1942 and only ever saw him again during a ten-minute visit to the Westerbork transit camp. Receiving no immediate news to the contrary in 1945 at the end of hostilities, she obviously hoped that he was among Auschwitz survivors liberated by the Russians, and wasn't told that he'd actually been murdered in KZ Flossenbürg until the following year. All she had left to remind her of Leo was a few boxes of race trophies and medals.

Emmy Steinweg moved back to Münster in 1950 and married an Austrian called Eugene Herzog three years later. This second husband died in 1973. Retaining her later married name, Emmy Herzog lived unremarkably until 1999. Then, already 96 years old, she wrote a book about her first love, '*Living with Leo – a fate under National Socialism*'. This was followed by a semi-autobiographical novel about four women growing up in Münster in the inter-war period, published in 2006. Emmy now lives in a Catholic old people's home and celebrated her 106th birthday on 13 April 2009. But like Leo, she never made it to the Isle of Man.

◆ Heinrich 'Heiner' Fleischmann returned to race for NSU after the war (facing page, left) and finally added a fourth German 350cc national championship to his curriculum vitae in 1950. He also famously beat Schorsh Meier and BMW's Kompressor on a blown 500 Rennmax in the last-ever event in which supercharged machines were allowed – held at the Sachsenring that year.

MOUNTAIN COURSE

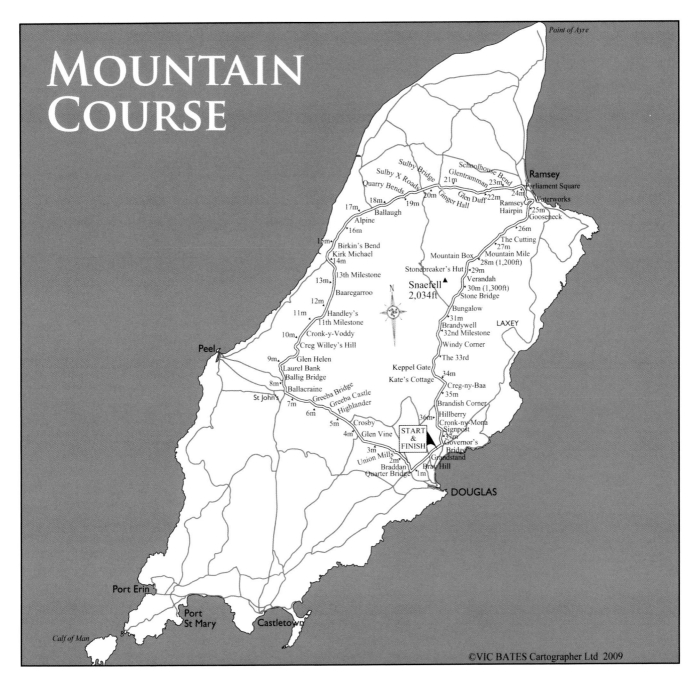

Point of Ayre

Sulby Bridge
Sulby X Roads
Quarry Bends
Schoolhouse Bend
Glentramman 23m
21m
Ramsey
Parliament Square
Glen Duff 22m
24m
Waterworks
20m
Ginger Hall
Ramsey
Hairpin
25m
Gooseneck
18m
17m
Ballaugh
19m
26m
Alpine
16m
The Cutting
27m
15m
Birkin's Bend
Kirk Michael
14m
Mountain Box
Stonebreaker's Hut
Mountain Mile
28m (1,200ft)
13m
13th Milestone
29m
Verandah
30m (1,300ft)
Stone Bridge
12m
Baaregarroo
Snaefell
2,034ft
11m
Handley's
11th Milestone
Bungalow
31m
Brandywell
32nd Milestone
Windy Corner
LAXEY
10m
Cronk-y-Voddy
Creg Willey's Hill
Peel
9m
Glen Helen
Laurel Bank
Keppel Gate
Kate's Cottage
The 33rd
34m
Creg-ny-Baa
8m
Ballig Bridge
Ballacraine
35m
Brandish Corner
St John's
7m
Greeba Bridge
Greeba Castle
Highlander
Hillberry
Cronk-ny-Mona
Signpost
36m
6m
Crosby
37m
Governor's
Bridge
5m
4m
Glen Vine
START
&
FINISH
Grandstand
3m
Union Mills
2m
Braddan
Quarter Bridge
1m
Bray Hill

DOUGLAS

Port Erin

Port
St Mary
Castletown

Calf of Man
8

©VIC BATES Cartographer Ltd 2009